World War II
Battles and Leaders

D0370020

World War II
Battles and Leaders

AARON R. MURRAY, EDITOR

DK Publishing, Inc.

LONDON, NEW YORK, MUNICH,
MELBOURNE, AND DELHI

DK PUBLISHING, INC.
Editor Madeline Farbman
Assistant Managing Art Editor Michelle Baxter
Senior Editor Beth Sutinis
Creative Director Tina Vaughan
Jacket Art Director Dirk Kaufman
Publisher Chuck Lang
Production Manager Chris Avgherinos
DTP Coordinator Milos Orlovic

MEDIA PROJECTS INC.
Executive Editor Carter Smith
Editor Aaron R. Murray
Writer Charles A. Wills
Project Manager James A. Burmester
Consultants Clifford J. Rogers, United States
Military Academy; Steve R. Waddell,
United States Military Academy
Designer Laura Smyth, Smythtype
Cartography Ron Toelke, Rob Stokes
Picture Researcher Erika Rubel
Copy Editor Glenn Novak

First American Edition, 2004
04 05 06 07 08 10 9 8 7 6 5 4 3 2 1

Published in the United States
by DK Publishing, Inc.
375 Hudson Street
New York, New York 10014

Copyright © 2004 DK Publishing, Inc.
All rights reserved under International and Pan-
American Copyright Conventions. No part of
this publication may be reproduced, stored in a
retrieval system, or transmitted in any form or
by any means, electronic, mechanical,
photocopying, recording, or otherwise, without
the prior written permission of the
copyright owner.

A catalog record for this book is available
from the Library of Congress.

ISBN 0-7566-0260-2 (pb)
ISBN 0-7566-0259-9 (hc)

Reproduced by Colourscan, Singapore
Printed and bound in China by
South China Printing Co., Ltd.

Discover more at
www.dk.com

*Halftitle: U.S. Marine at Okinawa, 1945. Title
page: British Lancaster bombers, 1943.*

CONTENTS

POLISH SOLDIER'S HAT

RUSSIAN NAGANT REVOLVER

GERMAN STICK GRENADE

GERMAN ANTI-TANK
MINE

FjG42 GERMAN
ASSAULT RIFLE

JAPANESE BATTLE FLAG

UNSTOPPABLE RUSH TO WAR

World War II was the most destructive conflict in history. The war lasted six long years, from 1939 to 1945. The fighting raged through Europe, Asia, and Africa, and across the world's oceans.

THE LEADERS OF THE ALLIED NATIONS
From left to right: Prime Minister Winston Churchill of Britain, President Franklin D. Roosevelt of the United States, and Premiere Josef Stalin of the Soviet Union at the Yalta Conference, February 1945. The leaders of the Allied nations often disagreed, but they were united in their fight against the Axis.

The war had many causes. One of the most important was that Germany wanted to take back land it had lost in World War I (1914–1918). The peace terms of that war had given much German territory to other countries, such as Poland and Czechoslovakia.

The Germans were angry at losing World War I. This anger made many Germans support the National Socialist (Nazi) Party. The Nazis were led by Adolf Hitler, who promised to win back the territory Germany had lost in World War I. Also, there were great economic troubles in the 1930s, with millions of people around the world out of work. Hitler and the Nazis promised to improve the daily lives of the German people.

Nazis were followers of "Fascism," a political system where the government strictly controls politics and the economy. Fascist leaders are dictators, who do not allow their people to have freedom. Three Fascist dictators came to power in the 1930s: Hitler, Benito Mussolini in Italy, and Hideki Tojo in Japan. These Fascist rulers built powerful armies and navies. They wanted to expand their nations by taking land from other countries. Their plans were opposed by the democratic nations, where people had freedom. The most powerful democracies were Great Britain, France, and the United States.

The Japanese intended to capture much of Asia. In the early 1930s they attacked China and took over a large part of her territory. The United States objected to this, but was not yet ready to go to war to stop Japan.

Next, Hitler began to seize land from neighboring countries. In 1936, his troops occupied the Rhineland on the French-German border. In 1938, Hitler began to take control of Austria and parts of Czechoslovakia. The democratic nations did not order him to stop because they hoped to avoid another great war. Some world leaders thought the Soviet Union would stop Germany's expansion.

The Soviet Union was ruled by Josef Stalin, head of the Communist Party. Like the Fascists, the Communists did not allow political freedom. In August 1939, Germany and the Soviet Union signed a treay, the Nazi-Soviet Non-Aggression Pact, promising not to attack each other.

In Europe, only Britain and France could stop Hitler now. These two countries became allies. They agreed to join forces if one or the other was attacked. They also promised to protect Poland if Hitler moved against that country. All the world watched, wondering what would happen next.

THE EMPEROR RECEIVES HIS MINISTER
Hideki Tojo (right), Japan's minister of war, bows to Emperor Hirohito. The emperor had little power and Tojo essentially ruled Japan.

THE GERMAN AND ITALIAN FASCISTS
Benito Mussolini (center left) seized power in Italy in 1922, eleven years before Adolf Hitler (center right) did the same in Germany. Mussolini called himself *Il Duce*; Hitler was known to the German people as *Der Führer*. Both of these terms mean "The Leader."

MILESTONES OF CONFLICT

1939–40

SEPTEMBER 1939 Germany and the Soviet Union invade Poland • Britain and France declare war on Germany

NOVEMBER 1939 Soviet Union invades Finland

APRIL 1940 Germany occupies Denmark and invades Norway • Naval battle of Narvik, Norway

MAY 1940 Germany invades the Netherlands, Belgium, and France • Winston Churchill becomes prime minister of Britain

JUNE 1940 British Expeditionary Force rescued from the beaches of Dunkirk, France • Germany completes conquest of Norway • Italy declares war on France and Britain • France, defeated, signs armistice with Germany

JULY 1940 Battle of Britain begins

SEPTEMBER 1940 Japan joins the Axis powers (Germany and Italy)

OCTOBER 1940 Italy invades Greece

NOVEMBER 1940 Franklin D. Roosevelt is reelected president of the United States

DECEMBER 1940 British forces in Egypt begin driving an invading Italian army back into Libya

KING GEORGE VI AND QUEEN CONSORT ELIZABETH MEET LONDONERS DURING THE BLITZ

1941

MARCH Axis counteroffensive pushes British forces back into Egypt • The United States Congress passes the Lend-Lease Act

APRIL Germany invades Yugoslavia and Greece

MAY Allies evacuate Greece as Germans take Athens • German airborne forces capture Crete • Italian forces in Ethiopia surrender to British • Royal Navy sinks German battleship *Bismarck* • British forces gain control of Iraq

JUNE Operation Barbarossa, the massive German invasion of the Soviet Union, begins

JULY British and Free French forces gain control of Syria

OCTOBER German forces begin unsuccessful drive to capture Moscow

DECEMBER Japan hits U.S. fleet at Pearl Harbor and attacks Wake, Guam, the Philippines, Hong Kong, Malaya, Dutch East Indies • U.S. declares war on Japan • Germany and Italy declare war on U.S. • Japan sinks British battleship *Prince of Wales* and battle cruiser *Repulse*

THE BATTLESHIP *ARIZONA* SINKS AT PEARL HARBOR

1942

FEBRUARY Singapore garrison surrenders to Japanese • Battle of the Java Sea

APRIL U.S. bombers hit Tokyo in Doolittle Raid

MAY Last U.S. outposts in the Philippines surrender • Carrier Battle of the Coral Sea

JUNE U.S. Navy wins major victory at Midway • Japanese land in Alaska • German forces launch offensive in Soviet Union • British garrison at Tobruk, Libya, surrenders to Germans

JULY First Battle of El Alamein, Egypt

AUGUST U.S. Marines land on Guadalcanal in the Solomon Islands • Churchill and Stalin meet in Moscow • Allied raid on coastal port of Dieppe, France, ends in disaster

SEPTEMBER Massive battle for Stalingrad begins • U.S. and Australian forces move against Japanese on New Guinea

OCTOBER Second Battle of El Alamein begins

NOVEMBER Operation Torch: Allied invasion of French North Africa

1943

JANUARY U.S. and Australian forces drive Japanese from New Guinea • German Sixth Army surrenders at Stalingrad, Soviet Union

FEBRUARY Germans launch Kharkov counteroffensive • Japanese forces abandon Guadalcanal • Casablanca Conference • U.S. suffers defeat at Kasserine Pass, Tunisia

CHARLES DE GAULLE REVIEWS FREE FRENCH
TROOPS IN LONDON

MARCH Battle of the Atlantic comes to a climax as the sinking of Allied ships by German submarines reaches its highest point of the war

MAY U.S. retakes Alaskan islands Attu, Kiska • German forces driven out of North Africa

JULY Soviets win major victory in Battle of Kursk • Operation Husky: Allied forces take Sicily • Mussolini's government falls in Italy

SEPTEMBER Italian government seeks peace, but Germans continue fighting in Italy • Allied forces land in southern Italy

NOVEMBER Churchill, Roosevelt, Stalin meet at Teheran, Iran • Soviets retake Kiev, Soviet Union • U.S. Marines land on Tarawa in the Gilbert Islands

1944

JANUARY Allies land at Anzio, Italy • Siege of Leningrad, Soviet Union, ends after 882 days

JUNE Rome falls to the Allies • D-Day: Allied forces land in Normandy, France • Soviets begin Operation Bagration: Major drive westward • U.S. Marines land on Saipan in the Marianas Islands • Naval and air battle of the Philippine Sea

JULY Hitler survives an assassination attempt by some of his generals • Allies begin breakout from Normandy

AUGUST Allied forces invade southern France • Paris is liberated • Unsuccessful uprising against Germans in Warsaw, Poland

CANADIAN TROOPS COME ASHORE AT
NORMANDY, FRANCE

SEPTEMBER Operation Market-Garden: Unsuccessful Allied attempt to drive into Germany via the Netherlands

OCTOBER MacArthur leads U.S. forces in return to the Philippines • Battle of Leyte Gulf—largest naval battle in history—fought off Philippines

NOVEMBER Roosevelt elected to fourth term as president

DECEMBER Battle of the Bulge begins: German forces launch surprise attack on Allied lines in Belgium

1945

JANUARY Germans turned back in Battle of the Bulge • Burma Road supply route to China re-opened • Soviets resume westward drive, taking Warsaw

FEBRUARY Soviets capture Budapest, Hungary • Stalin, Churchill, Roosevelt meet at Yalta in Crimea • U.S. Marines land on Iwo Jima

GENERAL MACARTHUR SIGNS THE JAPANESE
SURRENDER DOCUMENT

MARCH Manila, Philippines, falls to U.S. forces • Allied forces cross the Rhine • Japanese defeated on Iwo Jima • Massive U.S. air raid devastates Tokyo

APRIL U.S. forces land on Okinawa • German and Allied forces link up on the Elbe River, Germany • Soviets encircle Berlin • President Roosevelt dies and is succeeded by Harry Truman • Hitler commits suicide as Berlin falls

MAY VE (Victory in Europe) Day as Germany surrenders to Allies • British Fourteenth Army retakes Rangoon, Burma

JULY Japanese resistance on Okinawa ends • Churchill, Truman, Stalin meet at Potsdam, Germany • Clement Attlee is elected prime minister of Britain, succeeding Churchill

AUGUST U.S. drops atomic bombs on Hiroshima and Nagasaki, Japan • Soviet Union joins war against Japan • Japan agrees to Allied surrender terms

SEPTEMBER VJ (Victory over Japan) day as Japanese surrender

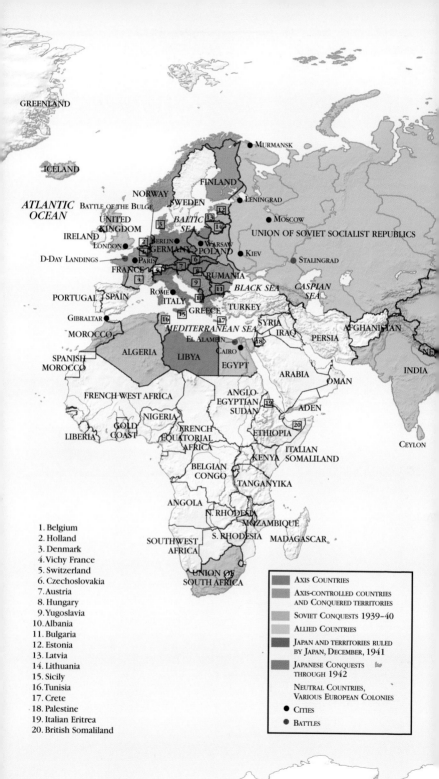

GREENLAND

ICELAND

ATLANTIC OCEAN

NORWAY
SWEDEN
FINLAND
MURMANSK
Leningrad
Moscow

IRELAND
UNITED KINGDOM
Battle of the Bulge
London
D-Day Landings
FRANCE
Paris
Berlin
GERMANY
Warsaw
POLAND
Kiev
Stalingrad

UNION OF SOVIET SOCIALIST REPUBLICS

BALTIC SEA

PORTUGAL SPAIN
Rome
ITALY
GREECE
TURKEY
BLACK SEA
CASPIAN SEA

Gibraltar
MEDITERRANEAN SEA
SYRIA
IRAQ
PERSIA
AFGHANISTAN

MOROCCO
SPANISH MOROCCO
ALGERIA
LIBYA
El Alamein
Cairo
EGYPT
ARABIA
OMAN
INDIA

FRENCH WEST AFRICA
ANGLO-EGYPTIAN SUDAN
ADEN
CEYLON

LIBERIA
GOLD COAST
NIGERIA
FRENCH EQUATORIAL AFRICA
ETHIOPIA
ITALIAN SOMALILAND
KENYA

BELGIAN CONGO
TANGANYIKA

ANGOLA
N. RHODESIA
MOZAMBIQUE
MADAGASCAR
SOUTHWEST AFRICA
S. RHODESIA
UNION OF SOUTH AFRICA

1. Belgium
2. Holland
3. Denmark
4. Vichy France
5. Switzerland
6. Czechoslovakia
7. Austria
8. Hungary
9. Yugoslavia
10. Albania
11. Bulgaria
12. Estonia
13. Latvia
14. Lithuania
15. Sicily
16. Tunisia
17. Crete
18. Palestine
19. Italian Eritrea
20. British Somaliland

AXIS COUNTRIES

AXIS-CONTROLLED COUNTRIES AND CONQUERED TERRITORIES

SOVIET CONQUESTS 1939–40

ALLIED COUNTRIES

JAPAN AND TERRITORIES RULED BY JAPAN, DECEMBER, 1941

JAPANESE CONQUESTS THROUGH 1942

NEUTRAL COUNTRIES, VARIOUS EUROPEAN COLONIES

● CITIES

● BATTLES

SIBERIA

ALASKA

ALEUTIAN ISLANDS

OUTER
MONGOLIA

MANCHUKUO

PACIFIC OCEAN

PEKING

KOREA

JAPAN

NAGASAKI

TOKYO

HIROSHIMA

CHINA

SHANGHAI

CHUNGKING

MIDWAY

FORMOSA

OKINAWA

IWO JIMA

HAWAIIAN
ISLANDS

BURMA

HONG KONG

PEARL HARBOR

RANGOON
SIAM

MANILA

SAIPAN

*SOUTH
CHINA
SEA*

PHILIPPINE IS.

GUAM

SAIGON

LEYTE

MAYLAYA

SINGAPORE

MARSHALL ISLANDS

TARAWA

BISMARCK SEA

RABAUL

GILBERT ISLANDS

SUMATRA

BORNEO

NEW BRITAIN

DUTCH EAST INDIES

NEW GUINEA

SOLOMON ISLANDS

PORT MORESBY

GUADALCANAL

NDIAN OCEAN

CORAL SEA

FIJI

AUSTRALIA

NEW CALEDONIA

SYDNEY

NEW ZEALAND

Nations Smashed in Lightning War

Germany invaded Poland soon after signing the non-aggression pact with the Soviet Union. Britain and France had promised to protect Poland, and now they declared war on Germany.

It was too late to stop Hitler, whose invasion rushed forward. Almost immediately, Soviet forces joined the attack, taking control of eastern Poland.

Poland was quickly defeated because Britain and France were not ready for war. Instead of launching an assault on Germany, they built up their defenses on the French-German border and waited for Germany's next move.

The people of the United States, led by President Franklin D. Roosevelt, watched this drama from across the Atlantic Ocean. Although the U.S. hoped to avoid war, most Americans opposed the fascist governments of Germany and Italy, which ruled their people with an iron hand.

RELOADING A HURRICANE
Royal Air Force (RAF) ground crew load ammunition into a Hawker Hurricane fighter. During the war, the outnumbered RAF fought the Luftwaffe for control of the skies.

September 1939	November 1939	April 1940	May 1940
Germans and Soviets invade Poland	Unsuccessful assassination attempt on Hitler in Munich, Germany	Germans invade Norway and Denmark	German Blitzkrieg in western Europe begins
U.S. declares neutrality	Soviet Union invades Finland		Belgium and the Netherlands fall

In April 1940, Germany launched several invasions, waging *Blitzkrieg,* "lightning war." First Denmark and Norway fell, then the Netherlands, Belgium, Luxembourg, and finally France. Most resisted bravely; all were swiftly defeated. In a six-week campaign, the once-mighty French Army was smashed. Italy's Fascist dictator, Benito Mussolini, was encouraged by Germany's spectacular success. He soon brought his country into the war on Germany's side against France and Britain.

At the end of 1940, Germany ruled much of western Europe. Britain was the only power that had the will and strength to resist. Led by Prime Minister Winston Churchill, Britain refused to surrender, even under heavy bombing by the German air force.

GERMAN TANKS IN PRAGUE
German tanks roll into the Czechoslovakian capital, Prague, in April 1939.

BLITZKRIEG!

The campaigns of the *Wehrmacht,* the German army, in 1939–1940 saw the development of a new style of warfare—*Blitzkrieg,* or "lightning war." Instead of advancing on a broad front with massed troops, fast-moving units of *panzers* (tanks) and motorized troops punched through the enemy's defenses, creating confusion and threatening the defenders from the rear. The powerful German air force, the *Luftwaffe,* supported the attacks. Often, airborne troops would drop by parachute to capture key points before the main attack.

ON THE GROUND
The Wehrmacht relied on well-trained infantry to gain final victory. This German throws a stick grenade at resisting Poles.

June 1940	July 1940	September 1940	October 1940
Allied troops evacuated at Dunkirk, France	British sink French fleet at Oran, Algeria	An Italian army invades Egypt	Italy invades Greece from Albania
France signs armistice with Germany	Battle of Britain begins	Japan joins the Axis	

A HOPELESS DEFENSE

On the night of August 31, 1939, Germany reported that Polish troops had fired on a German radio station on the Polish border. The "attack" had actually been faked by German troops to give Germany an excuse to invade Poland. At dawn on September 1, German forces smashed across the border.

Wehrmacht tanks and infantry quickly drove deep into Poland with the support of the bombers and fighters of the Luftwaffe. The bombers attacked Polish cities, including Warsaw, the capital. The Polish air force was taken by surprise. German bombers destroyed Polish planes on the ground before they could take off.

Polish troops defended their homeland with desperate bravery, but they were no match for well-trained German troops, supported by tanks and overwhelming air power. While German forces advanced rapidly, the Polish armies prepared to make a stand at Warsaw.

Then, on September 17, the Soviet Union joined the German assault on Poland. Stalin claimed

WARSAW IN FLAMES
German infantrymen watch the shelling and bombing of Warsaw, the Polish capital. Warsaw surrendered on September 27, but throughout the war a strong resistance movement in the city fought German rule.

STICK GRENADE
Advancing German infantry used stick grenades like this one. The long handle gave more leverage, allowing it to be thrown farther than regular hand grenades.

Losses
Polish:	60,000 killed, 910,000 prisoners
German:	13,981 killed, wounded unknown
Soviet:	Negligible

to be protecting Ukrainians and Russian minorities in eastern Poland, but this was just an excuse to grab territory. The Soviet Army poured across Poland's eastern border, trapping the remaining Polish forces in a vise. Warsaw held out for 10 more days against bombing and shelling that killed at least 40,000 civilians. The city's defenders finally surrendered to German forces on September 27. The last Polish troops laid down their arms on October 1, and Hitler and Stalin divided the country between Germany and the Soviet Union.

Poland, which had been an independent nation only since 1919—the end of World War I— now ceased to exist.

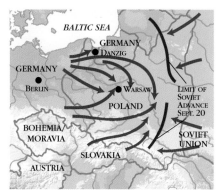

GERMAN AND SOVIET FORCES

UNDER ATTACK FROM ALL SIDES
Poland was bordered on every side by territory controlled by Germany and the Soviet Union. Polish defenders rallied against German forces moving on Warsaw, the Polish capital. Then Soviet forces moved in from the east, catching the Polish armies in a vise.

THE LEADERSHIP

HITLER ORDERED HIS GENERALS TO ACT with brutality in destroying Polish resistance, and to "close their hearts to pity." Stalin sent Soviet troops across the lightly defended eastern border, crushing all hope for the Polish defense.

WALTHER VON BRAUCHITSCH (1881-1948)
Born to a military family, Brauchitsch served as an officer in World War I. As commander in chief of the Wehrmacht, Brauchitsh planned the invasion of Poland and won great success in the beginning of the war. Hitler later removed Brauchitsch, blaming him for failure to defeat the Soviet Union in 1941.

"...the bravery and heroism of the ... Polish Army merits great respect."

—German general Gerd von Rundstedt

EDWARD SMIGLY-RYDZ (1886-1941)
A veteran Polish officer, Smigly-Rydz had fought against Russia in World War I and again in Poland's war with the Soviet Union in 1920–1921. Field Marshal Smigly-Rydz was commander in chief of Poland's armed forces when Germany and Russia invaded. He fled Poland as the German and Soviet forces closed in.

"A wheel always turns. This one will."

—Polish officer surrendering to the Germans

WOLF PACKS IN THE ATLANTIC

As an island nation, Britain imported food, fuel, and other materials needed to feed its people and keep its forces fighting. These supplies came by ship through the icy North Atlantic, where Nazi aircraft and warships waited to attack.

The deadliest warships of the *Kriegsmarine*, the German navy, were the submarines, or U-boats. U-boats operated in "wolf packs," which joined to attack when an Allied convoy, a group of cargo ships protected by warships, was spotted. Diving beneath the surface, the U-boats would slip into the midst of the convoy, fire their torpedoes, then escape before the warships could attack them.

By the middle of 1941, U-boats were causing terrible losses. Then the British broke the radio code that German headquarters used to communicate with their patrolling U-boats. The British navy now knew where the U-boats would strike next.

In December 1941, just as the United States entered the war, the Kriegsmarine realized what had

THE LEADERSHIP

BRITISH ROYAL NAVY COMMANDER RODGER WINN and U.S. Navy commander Kenneth Knowles led the Allies in the Battle of the Atlantic. Admiral Erich Raeder headed the German navy, while Karl Dönitz commanded the U-boats. Allied leaders gained an advantage when they broke the German code.

KARL DÖNITZ (1891-1980)
A loyal Nazi, Admiral Dönitz was the Kriegsmarine's submarine chief from 1935 to 1943, when he replaced Erich Raeder as commander in chief of the German navy. When Hitler committed suicide in April 1945, Dönitz succeeded him, soon surrendering to the Allies on May 7.

"I hope there are not too many like him."
—British officer after questioning a captured U-boat commander who had sunk 270,00 tons of shipping

RODGER WINN (1904-1972)
Commander Rodger Winn ran the Royal Navy's Submarine Tracking Room, a super-secret operation that gathered intelligence about U-boat movements in the Atlantic and elsewhere. He worked closely with his American counterpart, Commander Kenneth Knowles, head of the U.S. Navy's "Atlantic Section" Tracking Room.

"The only thing that ever really frightened me during the war was the U-boat peril."
—Winston Churchill

happened and changed its code. The U-boats again took a heavy toll on Allied shipping.

Allied codebreakers finally cracked the new German code in early 1943. This breakthrough and improved anti-submarine weapons soon led to heavy U-boat losses. By mid-1943, most of the surviving U-boats were withdrawn from the main Atlantic shipping routes.

······· MAIN ALLIED CONVOY ROUTES

SUPPLYING AN ISLAND NATION

Supply convoys sailed to Britain from major ports like Halifax, Canada, and New York, while others, from India, went around the tip of South America. Britain also held Gibraltar, the rocky southern tip of Spain, giving it access to the Mediterranean.

KRIEGSMARINE OFFICER'S CAP

About 41,000 German sailors served aboard U-boats during the war, and some 28,000 were lost at sea—the highest death rate of any service in World War II. Dönitz himself lost two sons on U-boats.

UP PERISCOPE!

A U-boat commander peers through a periscope, which allows him to view the surface while underwater. Submarines operated mainly on the surface, usually submerging only to attack or escape detection by Allied ships and aircraft.

Losses

Allies: 2,603 merchant ships, 175 warships, 200,000 crew killed

German: 769 U-boats, 28,000 crew killed

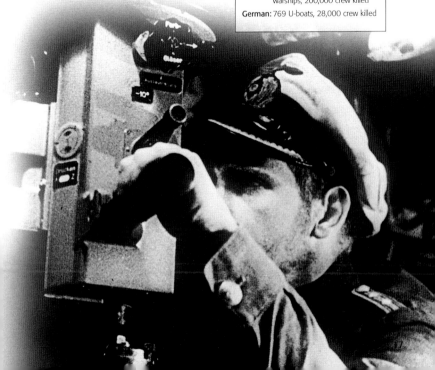

THE WINTER WAR

In October 1939, Stalin demanded that Finland give up a stretch of territory bordering the Soviet city of Leningrad. Although Finland was a small country, with a vastly outnumbered army, the Finnish government refused to give in. On November 30, Soviet troops invaded. To the world's surprise, the 33,000-man Finnish army held off a Soviet invading force of 100,000 troops. Eventually, the Soviets overwhelmed the defenders, while the Soviet air force bombed Finnish cities, including the capital, Helsinki. On March 12, the Finnish government agreed to the Soviet terms. Stalin's clumsy attack on Finland later led Hitler to underestimate the dangers of invading the Soviet Union.

RUSSIA INVADES
Soviet forces struck on the Karelian Isthmus, which separates Russia from Finland, and also at Petsamo in northern Finland.

▬ SOVIET FORCES
▬ FINNISH FORCES

"...the people of Finland earned for themselves the right to continue to live their own independent lives ..."
—Mannerheim on the Winter War

THE LEADERSHIP

STALIN HAD EXECUTED MANY SENIOR SOVIET OFFICERS in the 1930s, so his leaders were inexperienced. Field Marshal Mannerheim was a veteran commander who had fought in World War I and the Finnish Civil War.

CARL GUSTAV EMIL VON MANNERHEIM (1867–1951)
Field Marshal Mannerheim made a daring, but failed defense of his country against the Soviet Union. He later led Finnish forces that invaded Russia in cooperation with Nazi Germany in 1941. Mannerheim became president of Finland in 1944 and resigned in 1946.

THE WHITE DEATH
The Soviets were unprepared for the bitter cold of Finland's forests. Camouflaged in white, Finnish troops on skis easily slipped behind Soviet lines, ambushing supply columns and wiping out Soviet forces.

Losses
Finnish: 26,662 killed/missing, 43,557 wounded
Soviet: 100,000–200,000 killed/missing

SCANDINAVIA FALLS

On April 9, 1940, German forces invaded Denmark and Norway. Denmark surrendered quickly and without resistance. As German forces occupied southern Norway, Norwegian defenders were reinforced by British and French troops. On April 10–13, British warships sank German destroyers and transport ships carrying German troops to the northern port of Narvik. About 2,000 survivors made it ashore, but the larger Allied force drove the Germans out of Narvik. The Allied force was withdrawn in June as France approached collapse. With the Allies gone, the Germans soon overran the Norwegian defenders.

"Bands of Germans continued to drift through the town and up into the Fagernes Mountains …"

—Theodor Broch, mayor of Narvik

NORTHERN ADVANCE
The Germans attacked Norway to protect the supply of iron ore from Sweden. Iron ore was needed to make steel for the Nazi war machine. Allied forces fought to stop German landings in Narvik and Trondheim.

▬▬▬ GERMAN FORCES

▬▬▬ ALLIED FORCES

THE LEADERSHIP

GENERAL EDUARD DIETL'S LEADERSHIP during the Narvik campaign became a legend. He held his mountain troops together against a far superior Allied force and led them on a skillful retreat from Narvik.

EDUARD DIETL (1890–1944)
General Dietl was one of the best Nazi field commanders. After the Norwegian campaign, Dietl became commander of the Twentieth Mountain Army, fighting against Soviet forces. He was killed in a plane crash in June 1944.

MOUNTAIN MEN
Most of Dietl's troops came from the Wehrmacht's elite Third Mountain Division, some of whom are shown here crossing one of Norway's fjords (a narrow inlet of the sea between cliffs) aboard rubber boats.

This cloth badge of German Mountain troops shows the Edelweiss flower.

Losses

Allies: 6,365 killed (approximate figure)

German: 4,000–5,000 killed

WAR COMES TO LOWLANDS

Early on the morning of May 10, 1940, German paratroops and gliders swooped down to seize key positions along Germany's border with Belgium and the Netherlands. Achieving surprise, these daring operations opened up both countries to the invading Germans.

The Dutch held out for four days against the German assault. A Luftwaffe bombing raid on the city of Rotterdam left more than 800 civilians dead. As the Dutch fought to the north, French and British armies under the command of Maurice Gamelin moved into Belgium in a counterattack to stop the advancing Germans.

At the same time, seven German panzer divisions (a World War II German division was made up of 10,000–20,000 soldiers) smashed through the rugged forests of

ASSAULT FROM ABOVE
A German *Fallschirmjäger* (paratrooper) jumps from a Junkers J-52 transport aircraft over Holland. Airborne units quickly seized bridges and fortifications, including Belgium's massive Fort Eban Emael.

Losses
German: 100,000 killed, 100,000 wounded (approximate)
French: 600,000 killed/wounded/missing, 1 million prisoners (approximate)

Belgium's Ardennes region toward Sedan in France. This route lay to the north of the Maginot Line, the series of massive forts that the French high command believed would block any German invasion.

By May 14 most of the invasion force had crossed the Meuse River. French and British units counterattacked in places, but these actions were too weak and scattered to hold back the German advance. Wheeling west, the Germans drove toward the English Channel. This move divided the Allied defense into two isolated groups. Cut off from the rest of the Allied forces, the French First Army, together with the BEF (British Expeditionary Force, the 40,000-man army sent by Britain to fight in France and Belgium), and what was left of the Belgian army were all trapped along the coast.

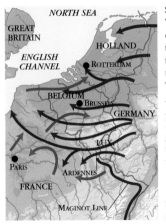

SICKLE STROKE
The Germans drove through the Ardennes forest toward France, and then to the coast. This move split the Allies, stopping the Allied forces in Belgium from going to the aid of the French forces to the south.

■ GERMAN FORCES
■ ALLIED FORCES

THE LEADERSHIP

THE GERMAN INVASION PLAN, code-named *Sichelschnitt* ("Sickle Stroke"), was largely the work of Fritz Erich von Manstein, chief of staff of the Wehrmacht's Army Group A. Hitler supported the plan, though many senior commanders thought it too risky.

"The confidence of the man in the ranks rests upon a man's strength of character."
—Manstein

FRITZ ERICH VON MANSTEIN (1887-1973)
A master of Blitzkrieg warfare, the Berlin-born Manstein went on to lead panzer units in many major battles in Russia. Despite winning promotion to field marshal in 1942, Manstein argued frequently with Hitler, who removed him from command. In 1950 he was sentenced to 18 years in prison for war crimes, but was released in 1952.

MAURICE GAMELIN (1872-1958)
French Army chief of staff from 1935 and commander in chief of the British and French forces facing the German invaders, Gamelin failed to meet the challenge of German Blitzkrieg. He was replaced by Maxime Weygand on May 20 and later spent two years (1943–1945) imprisoned by the Germans in Italy.

"Aucune." ("None.")

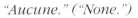

—Gamelin, when asked how many troops the French had in reserve on May 16

MIRACLE AT DUNKIRK

By the third week in May the Allied troops in Belgium were retreating toward the port of Dunkirk on the French coast. The Wehrmacht now had the chance to destroy them. On May 24, however, Hitler ordered his panzer divisions to halt the pursuit. Historians debate why Hitler issued this "stop order," but whatever the reason, it gave the Allies enough time to reach Dunkirk. There the surrounding terrain, crossed by rivers and canals, slowed the German tanks when they started to advance again on May 26. Still, the Allied forces were trapped at Dunkirk, with their backs to the English Channel. "Only a miracle can save the BEF now," wrote General Alan Brooke, a senior officer in the BEF.

The miracle began on May 26 when the British Royal Navy launched Operation Dynamo—the rescue of the BEF from Dunkirk. For nine days a fleet of some 887 vessels—including everything from warships to ferries, tugboats, and small yachts—braved attack by the Luftwaffe to transport the BEF to England. Some 217,000 British troops were evacuated by June 4, along with 110,000 French.

To the south, the Germans broke through the French defensive line—known as the Weygand Line after the new Allied commander—despite fierce resistance in many places. The French government fled Paris on June 10, four days before German troops reached the city. Soon afterward France's new premiere—84-year-old Henri Philippe Pétain, a hero of World War I—announced that France would seek an armistice, or peace agreement, with Nazi Germany.

A LONG, WEARY WAIT

Exhausted British soldiers line up on the beach at Dunkirk, waiting to board ships to take them across the English Channel. Poor weather and RAF fighters gave some protection from the constant attacks of the Luftwaffe, but German warplanes managed to sink several ships and caused casualties among the men awaiting evacuation.

Losses	
Allies:	338,226 evacuated, 68,000 killed/wounded/prisoners
German:	45,000 killed/wounded/prisoners (September 1939–July 1941)

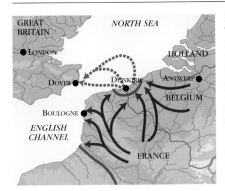

ESCAPE FROM DISASTER

The armored force commanded by Heinz Guderian had advanced past the French ports of Boulogne and Calais and was on the point of attacking the British, French, and Belgians at Dunkirk when ordered to halt. Allied forces were evacuated across the English Channel.

■■■■ GERMAN ATTACKS THROUGH JUNE 1, 1940

■■■■ ALLIED LINES MAY 28, 1940

▪▪▪▪▪ SEA EVACUATION ROUTES FROM DUNKIRK

THE LEADERSHIP

PANZER GROUP COMMANDER EWALD VON KLEIST, though personally somewhat cautious, had officers who included the aggressive Heinz Guderian and Erwin Rommel. Maxime Weygand was tough and determined, but by the time he took command the situation in France was going from bad to worse.

"We are all in splendid form."

—Erwin Rommel to his wife, June 1940

EWALD VON KLEIST (1881-1954)

General Kleist was recalled into service from retirement at the outbreak of World War II. After the fall of France Kleist took part in the invasions of Yugoslavia and Russia. He died in 1954 in a Soviet prison camp.

"In three weeks England will have her neck wrung like a chicken."

—Weygand to Pétain

MAXIME WEYGAND (1867-1965)

A staff officer in World War I and chief of staff of the French army from 1931 to 1935, General Weygand was 73 years old when he was called on to replace Maurice Gamelin. He had been serving as commander of French troops in Syria.

NEVER SO FEW

After the fall of France, Britain faced the Axis powers alone. Hitler began planning Operation *Seelowe* (Sea Lion), an invasion of Britain across the English Channel.

If this invasion was to have any chance of success, the German Luftwaffe had to defeat the Royal Air Force and win control of the skies over the Channel. The Luftwaffe offensive began in early July. Hundreds of German bombers and their fighter escorts attacked British aircraft factories, radar sites, and airfields.

Although the aerial battles took a heavy toll in pilots and planes for both sides, the RAF held on. The British had the advantage of radar, which gave them early

LUFTWAFFE INSIGNIA
Shown is a version of the flying eagle insignia which was worn on the jackets of Luftwaffe enlisted troops. The eagle holds a swastika, the ancient power symbol adopted by the Nazis.

THE LEADERSHIP

HERMANN GÖRING WAS NOT UP TO THE TASK of destroying Britain's air defenses. The RAF's Fighter Command—despite differences of opinion among commanders—rose to the challenge of defending Britain.

HERMANN GÖRING (1893-1946)
One of Germany's leading air aces in World War I, Göring was an early supporter of Adolf Hitler. He became commander in chief of the Luftwaffe in 1935. Arrogant, self-indulgent, and addicted to drugs, he seriously mishandled Luftwaffe operations during the war.

"The crew gazed down on the sea of flames in silence."
—German pilot on bombing Coventry, England

HUGH DOWDING (1882-1970)
Born in Scotland, Dowding joined Britain's Royal Flying Corps (later the RAF) in World War I. As chief of Fighter Command before World War II, Dowding greatly strengthened Britain's air defenses, building radar stations and reorganizing Fighter Command. Dowding provided brilliant leadership during the Battle of Britain.

"Never in the field of human conflict was so much owed by so many to so few."
—Churchill on the fighter pilots of the Battle of Britain

warning of approaching attackers. Also, many British pilots shot down over England or the Channel were rescued and quickly went back into action, while German pilots who parachuted from their planes were taken prisoner.

Early in September the Luftwaffe switched gears, launching massive daylight bombing raids against London in an effort to draw RAF fighters into combat. The RAF caused such heavy German losses that Hitler gave up this tactic, ordering night bombing instead.

In a period known as the "Blitz," the Luftwaffe continued to hit London and other British cities until May 1941, causing many civilian casualties.

BOMBING TARGETS
The Luftwaffe singled out London, Britain's capital, for punishment, but bombers also hit ports such as Liverpool and Portsmouth, and important industrial centers such as Birmingham and Manchester.

GERMAN TARGETS IN GREAT BRITAIN (SIZE INDICATES IMPORTANCE)

Occasional raids continued throughout the war, and in June 1944 Germany began launching V-1 flying bombs and, later, V-2 missiles at Britain, with London again the main target. About 60,000 British civilians were killed by German bombs and missiles during World War II.

SHADOW OVER LONDON
A German Heinkel He 111 bomber passes over London on September 7, 1940, "Black Saturday." This was the first day of the Blitz, the bombing offensive in which close to 2,000 civilians were killed.

Losses

British: 832 fighter planes lost, 507 aircrew killed

German: 1,268 planes lost, 3,363 aircrew killed, 2,641 prisoners

FIGHTING IN AFRICA

Italy declared war on France and Britain on June 12, 1940. Mussolini wanted to capture British and French colonies in Africa. Italian forces in the African nation of Ethiopia (Abyssinia), which Italy conquered in 1935–1936, moved against British-controlled territory in East Africa. By August Italian forces had occupied parts of the Sudan, as well as Kenya and British Somaliland (British Somalia).

In September 1940, the Italian army in Libya, an Italian colony in North Africa, launched an invasion of British-controlled Egypt. The Italian force, commanded by Marshal Rodolfo Graziani, numbered about 200,000 troops, while the British commander in Egypt, General Archibald Wavell, had only 63,000 men under his command.

Despite this advantage, the Italians halted three days later and dug in at Sidi Barrani, about 60 miles (97 kilometers) into Egypt. They were suffering from supply problems, because the British Royal Navy had won several major victories over the Italian Navy in the Mediterranean Sea. British control of the Mediterranean had made it difficult for the Italians to supply their units in Egypt.

DESERT DEFEAT
Some of the more than 130,000 Italian prisoners taken by the British during the Western Desert Campaign are led into captivity in Egypt.

Losses: Wavell's Offensive	
Allies:	476 killed, 1,225 wounded, 43 missing
Axis:	Killed/wounded unknown, 130,000 prisoners

26

Then, on December 9, the British Western Desert Force, 30,000 men led by General Richard O'Connor, set out to drive the Italians out of Egypt. This operation pushed the Italians back 400 miles (648 kilometers), taking the port of Tobruk, in Libya. By February 7, 1941, the British had captured the entire Italian Tenth Army.

A month earlier, in January 1941, a British force had won another victory, invading Ethiopia by way of the Sudan. In early April the British recaptured Ethiopia's capital, Addis Ababa, and the nation's exiled emperor, Haile Selassie, was back on his throne.

ITALIAN FORCES

BRITISH FORCES

THE WESTERN DESERT CAMPAIGN
Allied forces drove the Italians out of Egypt, then advanced along the coast of the Italian colony of Libya. In this successful offensive, the British captured thousands of prisoners.

THE LEADERSHIP

ITALIAN GENERAL GRAZIANI was a reluctant warrior who invaded Egypt only after pressure to do so from Mussolini. Wavell won a victory despite having little to work with. Hard-driving Richard O'Connor led Wavell's offensive operation.

RODOLFO GRAZIANI (1882–1955)
Graziani fought in Italy's wars of conquest in Africa (1908–1914) and in the 1930s served as a colonial ruler in Libya and East Africa. He managed to escape the defeat of his army in 1941 and continued to serve Mussolini until the Italian dictator's execution. He was imprisoned for war crimes in 1950.

"The loss of Egypt will be the final blow for Great Britain . . . ."
—Mussolini to Graziani

ARCHIBALD WAVELL (1883–1950)
General Archibald Wavell led no fewer than fourteen major operations in 1940–1942, from Egypt to Burma. Not all of them were successful, and Wavell was removed from command three times. He was viceroy (colonial ruler) of India (1943–1947) before that nation gained its independence from Britain following the war.

" . . . there were about five acres of officers and two hundred acres of other ranks."
—British officer's report on the great number of captured Italian troops

America Enters on the Allied Side

As the year began, Britain stood bravely against the might of ever-increasing Nazi power. Everywhere Hitler was on the offensive, and in the Pacific, Imperial Japan was a growing threat.

The bright spot in early 1941 was North Africa, where Allied forces defeated an Italian army that had invaded Egypt. Then Germany sent powerful reinforcements, under General Erwin Rommel, to help the Italians. A series of seesaw battles began in the desert and continued for many months. The Axis powers wanted to gain control of the Suez Canal in Egypt. The Suez was the vital route for shipping from Asia to the Mediterranean.

Spring 1941 also saw Axis conquest of Yugoslavia and Greece, pushing the Allied forces out of the Balkans.

Despite the Nazi-Soviet Non-Aggression Pact, Hitler had long planned an invasion of the Soviet Union. In June the Wehrmacht smashed eastward. Millions of Soviet

GERMAN GUNNERS ON THE RUSSIAN FRONT
The struggle between Germany and the Soviet Union was the biggest and perhaps most brutal of all the conflicts of World War II. Here, a German anti-tank gun crew fires on Soviet tanks in July 1941.

January	February	April	May
British capture Tobruk, Libya, from Italian forces	German Afrika Korps under Rommel arrives in Libya to reinforce Italians	Germany invades Yugoslavia and Greece	German forces capture Crete
			British warships sink German battleship *Bismarck*

troops were killed or captured in a series of great battles, but Hitler did not win the quick conquest he had hoped for. The Soviets managed to hold their key city of Leningrad, while a German drive on Moscow was halted as the bitter Russian winter set in. The Soviet Union had now joined the Allies.

On the other side of the world, Japan, now an Axis power, secretly prepared to attack United States and European possessions in the Pacific. On December 7, Japan attacked the American naval base of Pearl Harbor, Hawaii. The United States Pacific Fleet was shattered and America declared war on Japan; Germany and Italy declared war on America a few days later. Now the United States was at war on the Allied side.

THE FORTRESS OF TOBRUK
Stripped to the waist in the desert heat, a British gun crew defends Tobruk, Libya. By May 1941 the British were in retreat in North Africa, but they remained in control of Tobruk.

THE FLYING TIGERS

Even before Pearl Harbor, a small group of Americans was fighting Japan in the skies over China. In the spring of 1941, about 90 American military pilots volunteered to fly for the Chinese Nationalist government of Chiang Kai-shek, which was fighting Japanese invaders. Commanded by Colonel Claire Chennault, the unit, the American Volunteer Group (AVG), became better known as the Flying Tigers. The AVG returned to United States command in July 1942.

TIGERS OVER CHINA
A Chinese soldier stands guard over some of the AVG's distinctively painted Curtiss P-40 Tomahawk fighters.

June	September	November	December
Germany invades the Soviet Union	Germans begin siege of Leningrad	Germans take Kursk and Rostov	Soviets defending Moscow launch counterattack
	Germans take Kiev	German submarine sinks British aircraft carrier *Ark Royal* off Gibraltar	Japan attacks Pearl Harbor
			U.S. enters war against Axis

ENTER ROMMEL

The British success in North Africa was short-lived. A German force of armor and light infantry, the Afrika Korps, reached Tripoli in early February 1941 to aid the Italians. At the same time, the British forces were weakened by the transfer of several divisions to Greece to try to halt the German invasion there.

Just 40 days after the Afrika Korps landed, their dynamic commander, Erwin Rommel, launched an offensive. By mid-April he had pushed the British Western Desert Force back to the point from which they had started their attack into Libya in December 1940. Along the way the Italians and

Germans captured British general Richard O'Connor and trapped an Australian division in the port of Tobruk. A British counterattack, Operation Battleaxe, failed, largely because the German 88-mm gun (originally designed as an anti-aircraft weapon) proved to be devastating as an anti-tank weapon.

In July 1941, General Claude Auchinleck replaced Wavell, taking command of the Western Desert Force, which was now called the Eighth Army. In November, Auchinleck began an

AFRIKA KORPS CAP
This Afrika Korps cap featured a patch of the Imperial Eagle, national emblem of Hitler's Germany. The visor of the lightweight cotton cap gave protection from the sun's glare.

Imperial Eagle patch

TANK COUNTRY
The flat, open landscape of the Libyan desert made it easy for tanks (like the German Panzer Mark II shown here during Operation Battleaxe) to maneuver, but windblown sand could cripple engines.

Losses: Operation Crusader	
Allies:	18,000 killed/wounded
Axis:	38,000 killed/wounded

offensive in Operation Crusader, breaking through to Tobruk. Several months of stalemate followed.

Then in May 1942, Rommel again attacked Tobruk, forcing Auchinleck to withdraw after a fierce battle. On June 21, Tobruk surrendered to Rommel. The loss of this key port was a terrible blow to the British. However, Auchinleck received 300 Sherman tanks from the U.S., which helped make up for the great British losses.

MEDITERRANEAN SEA

TOBRUK

BARDIA

BENGHAZI

LIBYA

RETREAT TO
MERSA MATRUH

ALLIED LINES
APRIL–JUNE 1941

BRITISH LINES
MARCH 1941

EGYPT

AXIS FORCES

ALLIED FORCES

COASTAL COMBAT
Rommel drove the Allied forces out of Libya and back into Egypt, at the same time capturing the key port stronghold of Tobruk. The fighting in North Africa ranged over a narrow strip of land on the Mediterranean coast. Axis and Allied forces fought to control ports from where they could bring in vital supplies to keep their armies running.

THE LEADERSHIP

Rommel was admired by his Afrika Korps troops for his courage in battle. He sometimes personally led tank attacks. Wavell and Auchinleck were skillful commanders, but could not defeat Rommel.

CLAUDE AUCHINLECK (1884–1981)
General Auchinleck commanded British forces in India before replacing Wavell. When Auchinleck failed to defeat Rommel, Prime Minister Winston Churchill removed him from command. Auchinleck returned to command in India. He was promoted to field marshal after the war.

"To commit troops to a campaign in which they cannot be provided with adequate air support is to court disaster."

—Auchinleck

ERWIN ROMMEL (1891–1944)
Rommel was nicknamed the "Desert Fox" for his skill commanding armored divisions in North Africa. He later commanded German forces in France, but was accused by the Nazis of plotting to kill Hitler. Rommel had to commit suicide to save his wife and family.

"We have got Cyrenaica [part of Libya] back . . . It went like greased lightning."

—Rommel

AIRBORNE ASSAULT

By 1941 the nations of Bulgaria, Hungary, and Rumania (Romania) were allies of Germany. After pressure from Hitler, Yugoslavia also signed a treaty with Germany in March. The next day a group of Yugoslav military officers opposed to the treaty took control of the government. Hitler responded, ordering the bombing of Yugoslavia's capital, Belgrade, and launching an invasion on April 6.

Advancing German forces were helped by the fact that Yugoslavia's population was deeply divided along ethnic lines. Many Croats and Slovenes viewed the Germans as liberators from the Serbs, the majority group that controlled Yugoslavia. Although the Germans quickly took control of the country with help from Italy, Bulgaria, and Hungary, Yugoslav partisans (guerrilla fighters) resisted the occupation throughout the war.

Also on April 6, Germany invaded Greece to help Mussolini, whose Italian troops had been stopped by Greek forces in neighboring Albania. The outnumbered Greeks, and a British force of mostly Australian and New Zealand troops, fought bravely, but the capital, Athens, fell on April 27. In a "second Dunkirk," the Royal Navy evacuated 50,000 Allied troops to Egypt and the Greek island of Crete.

On May 20 German paratroops began dropping on Crete. Casualties were heavy; many Germans were killed before hitting the ground. The paratroopers, however, captured the Maleme Airfield, allowing reinforcements to be flown in aboard

Losses

Allies:	1,742 killed, 1,737 wounded, about 12,000 missing/prisoners
Axis:	1,915 killed, 1,632 wounded, 1,759 missing

FIERY ADVANCE
German vehicles roll through a Yugoslav village. As it had in Poland and France, the Wehrmacht used armor and aircraft to advance rapidly—so rapidly that Belgrade fell before much of the Yugoslav army could get into action.

transport planes. The Germans took the island after a week of heavy fighting, but the Royal Navy came to the rescue again, bringing 18,000 exhausted Allied survivors off the island. Though the Germans won victory, losses in the paratroop attack on Crete were so high that Hitler refused to allow any major airborne operations for the rest of the war.

BALKAN BATTLES
Nazi forces invaded through Rumania (Romania) and Bulgaria, which had joined the Axis. Resistance in Yugoslavia and Greece quickly collapsed. Allied forces were pushed south through Greece, then to the island of Crete, where they were finally evacuated under heavy attack.

███ AXIS FORCES
███ ALLIED FORCES

VICTORY BADGE
This armband was awarded to all German troops who had participated in the invasion of the island of Crete. The bulk of the awards were given to Luftwaffe paratroops.

THE LEADERSHIP

THE BRITISH COMMANDER ON CRETE, General Bernard Freyberg, believed the main German invasion force would come by sea, so he was slow to commit all his forces against the airborne troops. Freyberg's mistake gave the Germans a crucial advantage.

BERNARD FREYBERG (1889-1963)
Born in New Zealand, General Freyberg served in World War I. In that war, Freyberg was wounded many times, earning the Victoria Cross (Britain's highest military decoration for bravery). After commanding on Crete, he led New Zealand forces in North Africa and Italy.

"Like thousands of soap bubbles from a child's pipe."
—A New Zealand soldier describing the German paratroop drop

KURT STUDENT (1890-1978)
Luftwaffe general Kurt Student formed the Wehrmacht's first paratroop unit in 1938. In 1940, he took command of German airborne forces and directed Operation Merkury, the invasion of Crete. Student remained in charge of Germany's airborne forces for the rest of the war and commanded in Italy, France, and the Netherlands, and in the final defense of Germany.

"We began to despair of ever gaining our objectives or indeed of surviving at all."
—A German paratroop officer on Crete

AT THE RUSSIAN DOOR

Despite the 1939 Nazi-Soviet Non-Aggression Pact, Hitler had long planned to invade the Soviet Union, both to destroy the Bolshevik (Communist) regime and to seize land and resources for Germany.

Despite clear signs of a German buildup in eastern Europe and warnings from the British and from his own spies, Soviet dictator Josef Stalin refused to believe Hitler would turn on him. The Wehrmacht achieved complete surprise when the invasion—Operation Barbarossa—began on the morning of June 22, 1941.

Barbarossa was the biggest military operation in history. Three million men, in three Army Groups, hurtled into the Soviet Union. Army Group North advanced into the Baltic countries of Lithuania and Latvia, driving toward the Soviet city of Leningrad. Army Group Center advanced into Byelorussia (White Russia, now Belarus) toward Moscow. Army Group South aimed toward Kiev, the capital of the Ukraine.

The invaders met with success at first. Most of the Soviet air force was destroyed while still on the ground in the first days of the invasion. A series of massive battles in June and July brought the Germans many hundreds of thousands of Soviet prisoners.

In August and September, however, the Soviets rallied, often defending positions to the last man and sometimes even counterattacking. The Wehrmacht's supply lines were now stretched to the limit, and there were arguments in the German high command over whether to make Kiev or Moscow the main objective. With winter approaching, the easy victory Hitler had expected had escaped him.

GENERAL WINTER
With snow already on the ground, German troops advance through a village near Moscow in October 1941. The German high command expected victory before the first snowfall, so the troops faced the brutal cold of the Russian winter without proper uniforms and equipment.

Losses	
Soviet:	4.7 million killed/wounded/ prisoners/missing
Axis:	730,000 killed/wounded/ prisoners/missing

THREE-WAY THRUST
The Wehrmacht's invasion routes in Operation Barbarossa were planned, in part, to avoid the Pripet Marshes, a 40,000-square-mile (64,374-square-kilometer) swamp where rapid movement was impossible.

FINLAND
LENINGRAD
ESTONIA
LATVIA
MOSCOW
LITHUANIA
PRIPET
MARSHES
SMOLENSK
SOVIET UNION
POLAND
KIEV
ROSTOV
GERMAN
FRONT LINE
JUNE 22, 1941
BLACK SEA

■ AXIS FORCES

RUSSIAN REVOLVER
Special units of the NKVD (Soviet secret police) were often positioned behind the front line. They used revolvers such as this one to shoot Soviet deserters.

THE LEADERSHIP

FOR ALL ITS EARLY SUCCESS, BARBAROSSA soon proved to be a failure of German leadership. Quarrels between Hitler and his generals and between the generals themselves robbed the Wehrmacht of quick victory.

SEMYON TIMOSHENKO (1895-1970)
In 1941 Marshal Timoshenko was the Soviet Union's commissar (minister) of defense, but when Stalin personally took over that position, Timoshenko took command leading Soviet forces. He successfully defended Rostov, Ukraine, in November 1941. Timoshenko captured Vienna, the capital of Austria, in 1945.

"In the Soviet army it takes more courage to retreat than to advance."

—Stalin

FEDOR VON BOCK (1880-1945)
The commander of Army Group Center, Von Bock was a highly decorated veteran of World War I. He refused to take part in the July 1944 plot against Hitler—but he did not betray the plotters. He was killed with his family in an Allied air raid on Hamburg, Germany, in the last days of the war.

"You have only to kick in the door and the whole rotten structure will come crashing down."

—Hitler to his generals before the invasion

35

WINTER CLOSES IN

A month after Operation Barbarossa began, Hitler weakened the armies advancing toward Moscow, sending a strong armored force, commanded by General Heinz Guderian, south to help in the campaign to take Kiev, the capital of the Ukraine.

Most of the Wehrmacht high command disagreed with Hitler's order, believing that the best chance for victory was to defeat the Soviet forces defending Moscow and capture the capital. Hitler, however, wanted to destroy as much of the Soviet Army as possible, breaking Soviet resistance.

At a conference of the Wehrmacht high command on August 23, Hitler agreed to let Guderian's panzers join the attack on Moscow—but only after

Kiev was captured. By the end of September German forces had succeeded. Kiev had fallen, with 665,000 Soviet prisoners taken.

Operation Typhoon—the campaign to take Moscow—now began. By now rain had turned Russia's already poor roads into seas of mud, slowing the Axis advance. Still, by early December—when dropping temperatures froze the roads hard— Wehrmacht units had moved to within 20 miles (32 kilometers) of the capital.

On December 6, the day before the Japanese attack on Pearl Harbor, Georgi Zhukov, whom Stalin had put in charge of Moscow's defense, began a counterattack that drove back the frostbitten, exhausted Germans. Hitler ordered the army to go on the defensive, but refused to allow a full-

THE COUNTERATTACK
These Soviet troops are in the frontline of their great counterattack of December 1941. Reinforced Soviet armies pushed the Wehrmacht back from Moscow.

Losses	
Soviet:	514,338 killed/missing 143,941 wounded
Axis:	55,000 killed/wounded

RUSSIANS HIT BACK

Axis forces had advanced deep into Russia, threatening Moscow, the capital, and laying siege to Leningrad in the north. Then the arrival of reinforcements from Siberia and other areas allowed the Soviets to launch a powerful offensive in December, pushing back the Axis lines and taking the pressure off Moscow.

GERMAN ATTACKS NOV. AND DEC. 1941

SOVIET COUNTERATTACKS NOV. AND DEC. 1941

Box magazine can hold ten rounds of ammunition

TOKAREV SVT-40 RIFLE

This semi-automatic Soviet rifle could be loaded and fired faster than the bolt-action rifles used by many German and Soviet infantrymen. Soviets also made use of submachine guns, which were easy to produce in large numbers.

scale retreat. Blaming his generals for the failure to take Moscow, Hitler ordered a shake-up of the Wehrmacht high command, firing several top commanders and taking personal control of the army.

THE LEADERSHIP

HITLER'S REFUSAL TO LISTEN TO HIS COMMANDERS hampered the Wehrmacht's operations. Stalin kept tight control over his generals, but was sometimes willing to take their advice.

HEINZ GUDERIAN (1888-1954)

The author of a pioneering 1938 book on armored warfare, General "Hurrying Heinz" Guderian put his ideas into practice in France and Russia. Relieved of command after the failure to take Moscow, Guderian was recalled as the Wehrmacht's inspector-general of panzer troops in March 1943.

"We have severely underestimated the Russians, the extent of the country, and the treachery of the climate."

—Guderian, 1941

GEORGI ZHUKOV (1896-1974)

Zhukov survived Stalin's purges to become the leading Soviet commander of World War II. After successfully defending both Leningrad and Moscow, Zhukov won the decisive battle of Stalingrad in the winter of 1942–1943. Promoted to Marshal of the Soviet Union, he led the Red Army into Berlin in the spring of 1945.

"If we come to a minefield, our infantry attacks exactly as if it were not there."

—Zhukov

DAY OF INFAMY

By mid-1941 tensions were running high between the Empire of Japan and the United States. President Franklin Roosevelt had cut off exports of oil and metal to Japan to protest Japan's ongoing war with China and occupation of French colonies in Southeast Asia.

Japan's army and navy needed those resources for their plan to conquer Asia. Army officers wanted to attack the Soviet Union. Japanese and Soviet troops had already clashed in an undeclared war on the border between Mongolia and Manchuria. The navy, however, favored a "southern strategy," attacking United States and European territories in the Pacific. The southern strategy won out.

Japan's top admiral, Isoroku Yamamoto, had spent much time in America. Since early 1941 he had argued for a surprise raid to destroy the United States Pacific Fleet, based at Pearl Harbor, in the Hawaiian Islands.

Yamamoto said that only a "knockout blow" would give Japan enough time to expand its Pacific

THE LEADERSHIP

YAMAMOTO'S PLAN WAS DARING and Nagumo carried it out brilliantly, but Pearl Harbor was far from a complete success. Nagumo decided to turn the strike force back instead of seeking out and destroying the United States Pacific Fleet's aircraft carriers, which were at sea on December 7.

HUSBAND KIMMEL (1882-1968)
Pacific Fleet commander Admiral Husband Kimmel was blamed—perhaps unfairly—for the failure to anticipate the attack. He was removed from command, and a presidential commission in 1942 found him guilty of dereliction of duty.

"Yesterday, December 7, 1941—a date which will live on in infamy…"
—President Franklin Roosevelt's December 8 address to Congress

ISOROKU YAMAMOTO (1884-1943)
Admiral Yamamoto first saw action (and was wounded) in the Japanese Navy's victory over a Russian fleet at Tsushima, in 1905. A keen poker player, he carried his gambler's instincts into operations such as Pearl Harbor and Midway. He was killed when United States fighters shot down his plane over the Solomon Islands in 1943.

"I will run wild and win victory upon victory. But then, if the war continues…I have no expectation of success."
—Yamamoto, 1940

empire before the industrial might of America could be brought to bear.

The element of surprise was vital, and Admiral Chuichi Nagumo secretly assembled a strike force of six carriers and 360 aircraft. The Japanese force sailed for Pearl Harbor, Hawaii, on November 26, maintaining complete radio silence on their long voyage across the northern Pacific.

On the morning of Sunday, December 7, carriers launched the first wave of torpedo-bombers and dive-bombers. Despite being spotted by radar, the attackers arrived without warning. Many of the American sailors were still in their bunks. Within a couple of hours eight battleships and ten other vessels were sunk or sinking. About 200 aircraft were destroyed on the ground.

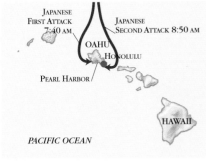

JAPANESE FIRST ATTACK 7:40 AM

JAPANESE SECOND ATTACK 8:50 AM

OAHU

HONOLULU

PEARL HARBOR

HAWAII

PACIFIC OCEAN

JAPANESE NAVAL FORCES   ● US NAVAL FORCES

BOMBING OF PEARL HARBOR
Admiral Nagumo's aircraft struck in two attack waves, the first wave at 7:40AM, the second at 8:50AM. Pearl Harbor, on the island of Oahu, in the Hawaiian chain of islands, was a key American naval base in the Pacific Ocean.

ABANDON SHIP
Sailors abandon the sinking battleship *California* during the Pearl Harbor attack. About 1,000 of the men killed at Pearl Harbor died aboard the battleship *Arizona,* which exploded after a direct hit.

Losses

U.S.:	2,403 killed, 1,178 wounded
Japanese:	100 sailors and aircrew killed (approximate)

The smoking battleship California *sinks at Pearl Harbor*

WINNING BACK BURMA

In December 1941 the Japanese Fifteenth Army invaded Burma (Myanmar) in Southeast Asia, where the British had only a small force. The loss of Burma threatened the Burma Road—the supply route for Chinese general Chiang Kai-shek's forces fighting the Japanese.

By April 1942 the Japanese had captured the Burma Road from the Chinese army that was defending it and had forced the British to retreat to India.

In late 1942 the British began a limited offensive operation in the Arakan region of Burma. Also, the "Chindits," a force specializing in jungle warfare, were sent behind Japanese lines to fight a guerrilla war. Led by brilliant British general Orde Wingate, the Chindits were a dangerous threat, outfighting the Japanese in the jungle.

In early 1944 the British Fourteenth Army, under General William Slim, made another offensive into Burma. A counterattack by the Japanese Fifteenth Army trapped part of Slim's forces in the towns of Imphal and Kohima. For four months the armies were locked in fierce battles. By July, the Japanese were defeated and forced to retreat.

LEDO ROAD PATCH

This patch shows a sun over a twisting road. It was worn by United States forces building the Ledo Road from Ledo, India to China. The Ledo Road ran through Burma, where it connected with the Burma Road.

THE FORGOTTEN FOURTEENTH

The British Fourteenth Army included Allied troops from India (shown here), Africa, and Britain. The Army was called the "Forgotten Fourteenth" because British leaders paid more attention to the action in Europe and North Africa than to the war in Burma.

Losses: Imphal and Kohima	
Japanese:	30,502 killed, 23,002 wounded
British:	2,700 killed, 10,000 wounded

Also in 1944, an American unit led by General Frank Merrill and nicknamed "Merrill's Marauders," marched behind enemy lines to fight with the Chindits against the Japanese. These two forces were successful, but suffered great losses.

On May 3, 1945, Allied armies recaptured Rangoon, Burma's capital. There were several more months of hard fighting, however, and only the final surrender of Japan on September 2, 1945, brought the long Burma Campaign to an end.

JAPANESE LINE JANUARY 1, 1944

INDIA
IMPHAL

CHINA

BURMA

BAY OF BENGAL

PROME

JAPANESE LINE JANUARY 1, 1945

RANGOON

SIAM

INDIAN OCEAN

ALLIED OPERATIONS 1944-1945
JAPANESE LINES 1944, 1945

RETAKING BURMA
Burma was won back from Japanese forces in a long, hard-fought campaign, lasting from 1941 to 1945. In 1944, Allied armies broke through Japanese defenses bordering India. American and Chinese forces attacked across the Chinese border. An attack was also made from the sea against the capital Rangoon, which fell to the Allies in May 1945.

THE LEADERSHIP

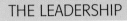

BRITISH ADMIRAL LORD LOUIS MOUNTBATTEN had an outstanding subordinate in General William Slim who turned the defeated British Fourteenth Army into a disciplined force. Mountbatten also worked with American general Joseph Stilwell.

LOUIS MOUNTBATTEN (1900–1979)
Head of the Allied South East Asian Command (SEAC), Mountbatten commanded that theater successfully from 1943 until the end of the war, working together with Chinese and American allies. Mountbatten later served as the last British ruler of India. He was murdered by Irish Republican Army terrorists in 1979.

"I tell you as officers, that you will neither eat, nor drink . . . until . . . your men have."
—General William Slim

RENYA MUTAGUCHI (1886-1966)
Known for his hot temper, General Mutaguchi led the 1944 offensive, code-named U-Go, which aimed to knock the British off-balance in Burma (and, he hoped, spark an uprising against British rule in India) by invading India's Assam Province. He was relieved of command following U-Go's failure. British authorities later accused him of war crimes, but the charges were dropped for lack of evidence.

"Retreat, and I'll court-martial you."
—Mutaguchi to his subordinate commander, at Kohima

On the Road to Victory

1942

The high tide of German and Japanese conquest came in 1942, but so also did the first major victories for the Allies. That summer, the Allies won the advantage and started on the road to victory.

In the Pacific, the news was all bad for the Allies in the first half of 1942. The Japanese drove the United States from the Philippines, the Dutch from the East Indies (Indonesia), and the British from Burma, Malaya (Malaysia), and Singapore. Japanese forces landed in New Guinea, threatening Australia.

Then, in May, the United States Navy stopped a Japanese force in the Battle of the Coral Sea. In June came the turning point, a great American victory at the island of Midway. After Midway, the United States began a counteroffensive. The strategy behind this offensive was called "island hopping." American forces moved toward Japan, capturing key islands along the way, and bypassing others,

AMERICAN TROOPS IN CORREGIDOR
The strain of being under siege can be seen in the faces of these American soldiers in a tunnel on Corregidor, an island in Manila Bay, Philippines, that held out against the Japanese invaders until May 1942.

January	February	April	May
Soviets retake Kiev	Singapore falls to Japan	U.S. bombers raid Japan in the Doolittle Raid	Battle of the Coral Sea
Japanese forces invade Burma			Last U.S. forces in Philippines surrender

leaving them isolated. By August, the offensive had started. American forces landed in the Solomon Islands.

On the Russian front, despite severe German losses and the growing strength of the Soviet Army, Hitler was determined to defeat the Soviet Union. He ordered the Wehrmacht to advance to the Volga River and take the city of Stalingrad—but by the end of 1942 an entire German army was trapped in the ruins of that city.

In North Africa, the British suffered a defeat when Tobruk fell in June, but in October and November the British Eighth Army defeated Axis forces under Rommel, at El Alamein. Days later a United States-British invasion force landed at several places along the coast of French-ruled North Africa. As the year ended, Japan and Germany were finally on the defensive.

YELLOW STAR

TOWARD STALINGRAD
A German gun crew is shown during the summer 1942 offensive. By May the Germans had lost over a million men killed or captured.

THE HOLOCAUST

From 1942, the Nazi regime forced Jews of Europe to wear a yellow star, allowing authorities to identify them. The Nazis made anti-Semitic laws that restricted Jews. In January 1942, Nazi leaders met at Wannsee, near Berlin, and decided on the "final solution of the Jewish question": the complete extermination of Europe's Jews. By the end of the war 6 million Jews were dead, some starved and worked to death as slave laborers, others killed by poison gas in concentration camps.

WARSAW GHETTO
Jews of the Warsaw, Poland, ghetto bravely rose up against the Nazis in 1943, but the uprising was put down.

June	August	September	November
Battle of Midway	U.S. Marines land on Guadalcanal	Battle of Stalingrad begins	British victorious at El Alamein
Germans capture Tobruk, Libya	Allied raid on Dieppe, France		Allied landings in North Africa

JAPANESE TIDE ROLLS ON

Japan's raid on Pearl Harbor was part of a coordinated effort to expand its empire in Asia. In the days and weeks following December 7, 1941, Japanese forces captured the United States-held islands of Wake and Guam, the British colony of Hong Kong on the South China coast, and the oil-rich Dutch East Indies (Indonesia).

On December 8, 1941, a Japanese force moved onto the Malay Peninsula (Malaysia) with the great port of Singapore as its objective. The British commander in Malaya, Sir Arthur Percival, had more than 100,000 men under his command. Although the defenders outnumbered the Japanese, they were a hastily assembled jumble of troops from across the British Empire, many of them barely trained.

Unable to stop the Japanese Twenty-fifth Army, the British retreated into Singapore at the end of January 1942. When Japanese units crossed the mile-wide Strait of Johore and gained a foothold on Singapore itself, Percival surrendered on February 15 and went into captivity with 130,000 men. It was the worst British defeat in history.

Also on December 8, Japanese planes bombed airfields in the Philippines, destroying planes on

THE LEADERSHIP

ALTHOUGH GENERAL PERCIVAL was not entirely to blame for the loss of Singapore, his failure to move decisively against the Japanese invaders contributed to the disaster. The Japanese commander, General Tomoyuki Yamashita, on the other hand, was willing to act boldly and take risks—despite the defenders' superior numbers.

"I came through . . . and I shall return."
—MacArthur upon arriving in Australia from Bataan

DOUGLAS MACARTHUR (1880–1964)
Vain but brilliant, instantly recognizable by his sunglasses and corncob pipe, MacArthur made good in 1944–1945 on his promise to reconquer the Philippines. He later oversaw the American occupation of Japan. MacArthur commanded United States forces in the Korean War before being relieved by President Harry Truman in 1951. His military career spanned a half-century.

"Japanese forces, using . . . bases at Singapore, can chase the British Navy into the Mediterranean."
—Admiral Tanetsuga Sosa

MASAHARU HOMMA (1888–1946)
General Homma commanded the main Japanese invasion force on Luzon. After the war he was executed for causing the deaths of thousands of United States and Filipino prisoners in the Bataan Death March.

the ground. Two days later Japanese troops began landing on the main Philippine island of Luzon.

The United States commander in the Philippines, General Douglas MacArthur, led 80,000 American and Filipino troops on a fighting retreat into the Bataan Peninsula. They were unable to receive supplies and reinforcements, and the troops on Bataan were soon starving. In early March 1942, President Roosevelt ordered MacArthur to escape to Australia. A month later General Edward King surrendered on Bataan. On May 6, 1942, the last United States position, the rocky island of Corregidor in Manila Bay, fell to the Japanese.

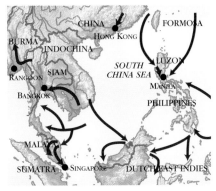

■■■■ JAPANESE INVASIONS DECEMBER 1941–MAY 1942

JAPAN GRABS FOR EMPIRE
After the strike on Pearl Harbor, Japan moved rapidly to capture as much territory as possible. Launching attacks that had been planned far ahead of time, Japanese forces were unstoppable as they won victory after victory in the Pacific.

JAPANESE TANKS IN MANILA
Here Japanese tanks roll into Manila, the capital of the Philippines. Before retreating into Bataan, MacArthur declared that Manila was an "open city." He hoped to spare the civilian population from Japanese attack. Japanese planes bombed the city anyway.

Losses: The Toll in Prisoners

Singapore:	130,000 British, Indian, Australian, and other troops
Philippines:	9,300 U.S. and 45,000 Filipinos (captured on Bataan)

FIRST STRIKE AT JAPAN

America wanted to strike back against Japan after Pearl Harbor, but the only way to get United States bombers within range of Japan's home islands was by sea. On April 2, the carrier *Hornet* sailed out of San Francisco

> *"They'll need a lot of luck."*

—Admiral William Halsey referring to Doolittle's force

with sixteen United States Army Air Force B-25 bombers aboard. The plan was for the bombers to be launched from the deck of the *Hornet* when the ship was 500 miles (805 kilometers) from Japan. They would fly on to China after dropping their bombs. When a Japanese ship spotted the *Hornet* 650 miles (1,046 kilometers) off the coast of Japan, Doolittle ordered the bombers launched. Thirteen of the bombers raided Tokyo, Japan's capital; three bombed other cities. The raid did little damage, but raised America's spirits and embarrassed the Japanese.

• • • • • Doolittle's Bombers
✱ Doolittle's Main Targets

AIR STRIKE ON TOKYO, JAPAN
USS *Hornet* came within 650 miles (1,046 kilometers) of Japan, then launched its bombers in a surprise attack on Tokyo.

THE LEADERSHIP

"Jimmy" Doolittle won the Congressional Medal of Honor and promotion to general for his leadership of the raid.

JAMES HAROLD DOOLITTLE (1896–1993)
Doolittle was already famous as a test pilot and air racer before the raid on Japan. He went on to command the Eighth Air Force in Britain and later fought in the Pacific. After the war he became a vice president of the Shell Oil Company and advised the United States government and military on aviation matters.

OFF THE DECK
A B-25 lumbers into the air. Planes of this size had never before taken off from the deck of a carrier. Many bombers ran out of fuel and crash-landed in China, some in Japanese-controlled territory. One B-25 landed in the Soviet Union and the crew was taken prisoner.

Losses
3 U.S. airmen killed in crash landings
8 captured by Japanese forces in China
(3 were later executed and 1 died of illness)

CLASH OF CARRIERS

In the spring of 1942 Admiral Yamamoto began a series of operations to keep the United States Navy out of the southwest Pacific. In April, Japanese forces successfully landed in the Solomon Islands, while another task force commanded by Vice Admiral Shigeyoshi Inouye steamed toward New Guinea. The United States

> *"Dixon to carrier, scratch one flattop!"*
>
> —Squadron leader Robert Dixon reports sinking the *Shoho*

Navy reacted, sending a carrier force to the Coral Sea. In a two-day battle, Navy and Marine pilots sank the Japanese light carrier *Shoho* and damaged the larger carriers *Shokaku* and *Zuikaku,* while Japanese pilots hit the American carriers *Lexington* and *Yorktown,* sinking the *Lexington* and seriously damaging the *Yorktown.* Although the losses in planes and ships were roughly equal, the Japanese had to abandon the operation against New Guinea.

PACIFIC OCEAN

RABAUL
NEW GUINEA
SOLOMON ISLANDS
GUADALCANAL
CORAL SEA
AUSTRALIA

ALLIED ATTACKS APRIL 28–MAY 4
JAPANESE ATTACKS APRIL 28–MAY 4

BATTLE OF THE CORAL SEA
In a great clash of navy air forces, the United States and Japanese fleets both sent their planes to attack the enemy's ships.

THE LEADERSHIP

Coral Sea was the first naval battle fought entirely by aircraft; the opposing ships never came within sight of each other. The naval commanders had to anticipate when and where the enemy would strike.

FRANK JACK FLETCHER (1885–1973)
Admiral Fletcher commanded United States naval forces at the Battle of the Coral Sea. He also fought in the Battle of Midway and commanded the invasion fleet that landed Marines on Guadalcanal.

LOSS OF THE *LEXINGTON*
The *Lexington*'s sailors abandon ship, to be picked up by supporting vessels. The "Lady Lex" was hit by two Japanese torpedoes and three bombs; she finally sank when an uncontrollable fire broke out below deck.

Losses	
Japanese:	1 carrier, 1 cruiser, 1 destroyer sunk; 1 carrier damaged
U.S.:	1 carrier, 1 destroyer sunk; 1 carrier damaged

TURNING POINT IN THE PACIFIC

The Doolittle Raid and the Battle of the Coral Sea convinced Admiral Yamamoto that he needed to destroy the United States Navy's carriers in order to safeguard Japan's home islands and complete Japan's Pacific conquests. Once again, Yamamoto gambled on a "knockout blow"—an attack on United States-held Midway Island, 1,200 miles (1,931 kilometers) northwest of Hawaii, which Yamamoto hoped would lure the American carriers into decisive battle.

The United States Navy in the Pacific had only three carriers and 180 planes available for action, against four Japanese carriers and 272 planes. Still, the Americans had an important advantage. Before World War II started, United States codebreakers had cracked Japan's secret communications code, which the American codebreakers called "Magic." As Yamamoto's fleet moved against Midway, United States naval commanders knew he was coming.

On June 4 Japanese carrier planes bombed Midway. Land-based planes from Midway attacked the Japanese carriers, but they failed to do any damage and suffered heavy losses. Torpedo bombers from the United States carriers *Hornet, Enterprise,* and *Yorktown* also attacked the Japanese. All were shot down, but dive-bombers from the *Yorktown* and *Enterprise* escaped the Japanese fighters. They arrived over the Japanese carriers while their decks were crowded with planes, bombs, and fuel. In just five

DIVE-BOMBERS ATTACK
Douglass SBD-3 Dauntless dive-bombers during Midway. The rugged Dauntless carried a crew of two and a 1,200-pound bomb load. All told, SBD-3s sank five Japanese carriers at Coral Sea and Midway.

Losses	
U.S.:	307 sailors and aircrew
Japanese:	2,500 (approximate)

minutes, three Japanese carriers—the *Akagi, Kaga,* and *Soryu*—were aflame and sinking.

Later that day planes from the remaining Japanese carrier, the *Hiryu,* damaged the *Yorktown,* which was later sunk by a Japanese submarine. The *Hiryu* itself was then sunk by planes from the *Enterprise.*

Shocked by the loss of his main carrier force, Yamamoto canceled the planned landing on Midway and withdrew his surviving vessels. Midway marked the turning point in the Pacific; from then on, the Japanese would be mostly on the defensive.

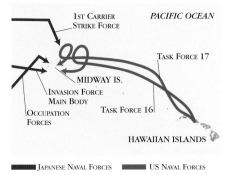

1ST CARRIER STRIKE FORCE
PACIFIC OCEAN
TASK FORCE 17
MIDWAY IS.
INVASION FORCE MAIN BODY
OCCUPATION FORCES
TASK FORCE 16
HAWAIIAN ISLANDS

■ JAPANESE NAVAL FORCES   ■ US NAVAL FORCES

DESTRUCTION OF THE JAPANESE CARRIERS
As a Japanese invasion force moved to invade Midway island, four carriers sent their planes to hit American defenses on the island. At the same time American planes took off to attack the Japanese carriers. The battle lasted four long days.

THE LEADERSHIP

ADMIRAL CHESTER NIMITZ planned and carried out the Battle of Midway, but he relied on cool-headed subordinates such as Admiral Raymond Spruance, who gave the order for an all-out air attack that sank the Japanese carriers.

CHUICHI NAGUMO (1886-1944)
Although Yamamoto chose Nagumo to command Japan's carrier fleet in April 1941, the admiral was a destroyer expert rather than an aviator. Despite the defeat at Midway, he remained in command of Japan's remaining carriers until November 1942. He committed suicide on Saipan in July 1944.

". . . we can succeed in drawing out the enemy's carrier strength and destroying it."
　　　　　　　—Yamamoto

CHESTER W. NIMITZ (1885-1966)
The leading United States admiral of World War II, Texas-born Chester Nimitz entered the Naval Academy when he could not get into West Point. As commander in chief of the United States Pacific Fleet and commander of the Central Pacific Area, Nimitz proved a master at combining carriers, submarines, and surface ships to counter and finally defeat the Japanese Navy. After the war he served as chief of naval operations.

"It is the function of the Navy to carry the war to the enemy so that it will not be fought on U.S. soil."
　　　　　—Nimitz

DEATH OF AN ARMY

After the failure to take Moscow and Leningrad in 1941, Hitler shifted the offensive to the south, with the Caucasus oil fields as the objective. Stalingrad, an important industrial city on the Volga River, soon became the focus of the southern campaign. Hitler hoped the fall of Stalingrad, named after Premiere Josef Stalin, would lower Soviet morale. For the same reasons, the Soviet high command was determined to hold the city at all costs.

The German Sixth Army, supported by Romanian, Hungarian, and Italian units, fought its way into Stalingrad in early September. The Germans managed to push the defenders into a narrow pocket along the west bank of the Volga River. From the east bank, however, the Soviets poured in supplies and reinforcements. For two months both sides slugged it out at close quarters, fighting from street to street, house to house, factory to factory.

In November the Soviets launched a counterattack, and by November 22 the Sixth Army was surrounded. German commander Friedrich Paulus and most of his men might have been able to break out, but Hitler ordered him to hold out. Luftwaffe chief Hermann Göring claimed he could keep the trapped army supplied by air, but only a fraction of the needed supplies made it through.

A force commanded by Erich von Manstein tried, unsuccessfully, to break through the Soviets and link up with the Sixth Army. By the end of the year Paulus's situation was hopeless. Finally, on February 2, he surrendered. Combat, hunger, disease, and frostbite had reduced the Sixth Army from 250,000 men to fewer than 100,000. The epic battle marked the turning point on the eastern front.

WAR OF THE RATS

Soviet infantry advance on a German position. Stalingrad was leveled by shells and bombs, and much of the fighting took place in the rubble, or underground—combat the Germans called *Rattenkrieg,* or "the war of the rats."

Losses	
Soviet:	500,000 killed (approximate)
Axis:	147,000 killed, 91,000 captured (approximate)

Rifle scope for deadly accuracy

SOVIET OFFENSIVE NOVEMBER 1942-JANUARY 1943
GERMAN RELIEF ATTEMPT DECEMBER 12-19, 1942

GERMAN K98 SNIPER RIFLE

THE SIXTH ARMY IS SURROUNDED

The Soviet forces smashed through Axis defenses and surrounded the German Sixth Army in Stalingrad. German forces tried to break through to relieve the Sixth Army, but the Soviets pushed them back.

THE LEADERSHIP

THE TEAM OF SOVIET MARSHAL GEORGI ZHUKOV AND GENERAL V. I. CHUIKOV was a potent combination. Chuikov was in charge of Stalingrad's defense, while Zhukov planned and directed the operation that encircled the Sixth Army.

"There will be no more field marshals in this war."

—Hitler, on hearing of Paulus's surrender

FRIEDRICH PAULUS (1890–1957)
Hitler promoted Paulus to field marshal in January 1943 hoping that he would commit suicide rather than surrender. No German field marshal had ever surrendered his army. After Stalingrad, Paulus collaborated with his Soviet captors by joining the "Committee of Free German Officers."

"There is only one road, the road that leads forward. Stalingrad can be saved by you, or wiped out with you."

—Chuikov to his troops at Stalingrad

VASILI IVANOVICH CHUIKOV (1900–1982)
Like his commander, Zhukov—indeed, like most Soviet generals—Chuikov was a very tough and determined officer. In the spring of 1945 he led the Soviet drive to Berlin and personally accepted the city's surrender. After the war he served as commander of Soviet occupation forces in Germany until 1953.

BOMBING THE REICH

After World War I, military planners had studied how air power could be the key to victory in future wars. Bombing industries and transportation networks would cripple the enemy government's ability to wage war. Bombing cities and killing and terrorizing civilians would break the enemy people's will to fight.

The Axis and Allies used both strategies in World War II. Britain's Royal Air Force (RAF) began large-scale "strategic bombing" on Germany and German-occupied Europe early in the war. Luftwaffe fighters and anti-aircraft guns shot down so many RAF bombers, however, that the British soon restricted their raids to nighttime. The RAF discovered that most of the bombs they dropped did not fall anywhere near their targets. Bombing continued anyway in the belief that "area bombing" would shake the morale of the German people.

In August 1942, the United States Eighth Air Force joined the bombing campaign. Taking off from bases in Britain, American B-17 Flying Fortresses and B-24 Liberators operated in daylight. Instead of "area bombing," they chose specific targets. Losses were also heavy for the United States until the arrival of the P-51 fighter in December 1943. The P-51

THE LEADERSHIP

THE UNITED STATES "MIGHTY EIGHTH" AIR FORCE— was commanded by General Ira C. Eaker from January 1942 to January 1944, when General James Doolittle took over.

ARTHUR HARRIS (1892–1984)
Leader of Bomber Command from February 1942 on, the gruff, single-minded British air marshal "Bomber" Harris remained convinced of the value of hitting Berlin and other cities even as RAF casualties reached crisis levels in 1941–1942.

". . . people say that bombing cannot win the war. My reply . . . is that it has never been tried . . . and we shall see."

—Harris, 1942

ALBERT SPEER (1905–1981)
Hitler put Speer, an architect, in charge of German war production in 1942. Despite the nonstop Allied bombing, under Speer's direction German production of tanks, planes, and other weapons actually rose in 1943, partly by using forced labor from German-occupied nations and from concentration camps.

" . . . the effects of aerial warfare are terrible . . . but one has to accept them."

—Göring after the Allied bombing of Cologne, May 1942

escorted bombers all the way to Berlin and back, protecting them from enemy fighters.

Allied bombing had a terrible effect on the cities. Raids such as those on Hamburg in 1943 and Dresden in 1945 caused "firestorms" that set the cities alight. These raids claimed thousands of lives, but did not break the German will to continue the war.

Direction finder

Powerful lenses

✳ PRIMARY ALLIED BOMBING TARGETS IN GERMANY

▬▬▬ V-1 ROCKET SITES 1944

● V-2 ROCKET SITES 1944–1945

BOMBING CITIES AND ROCKET SITES
The Allied bombing was heavy in the Ruhr and Saar regions, home to German industry. The Allies also tried to knock out the V-1 and V-2 rocket launch sites, hoping to stop these weapons, which were smashing into London.

SCANNING THE SKIES
Luftwaffe anti-aircraft gunners used powerful binoculars to search for Allied bombers. The Germans and the Allies also used the new technology of radar to detect incoming aircraft.

TARGET: GERMANY
British Lancaster bombers on their way to Germany in 1942. The best RAF heavy bomber of the war, the Lancaster had a crew of seven, could carry up to 14,000 pounds of bombs (or a single 22,000-pound "Grand Slam" bomb), and mounted eight machine guns for defense.

Losses
RAF Bomber Command: 55,000 killed, 40,000 wounded/prisoners.

US Eighth Air Force: 26,000 killed, 21,000 wounded/prisoners

THE MARINES HAVE LANDED

In June 1942 Japanese troops landed on Guadalcanal in the Solomon Islands of the South Pacific. They were there to build an airfield; if they succeeded, Japan would have control of the skies for hundreds of miles around. So began a six-month struggle in the air and on land and sea to win control of this 2,047-square-mile (4,023-square-kilometer) island of jungles, hills, and swamps.

The 19,000 men of the First Marine Division landed on Guadalcanal and two nearby islands on August 7 and quickly gained control of the airfield, which they named Henderson Field after a Marine pilot killed at Midway.

Palm fronds for camouflage

The next night, however, Japanese warships struck at the invasion fleet off Savo Island, sinking four American cruisers. The remainder of the invasion fleet withdrew, leaving the Marines on Guadalcanal with few supplies and no naval support or air cover. Japanese warships were soon transporting reinforcements to Guadalcanal, while the Japanese navy and aircraft shelled and bombed Henderson Field repeatedly.

JAPANESE HELMET
The soldier who wore this steel helmet twisted palm frond cuttings through the net in order to blend in with tropical foliage. Japanese infantry were skilled, determined jungle fighters, but the Marines proved their equal.

PEACEFUL BEACH
The First Marine Division's landing was mostly unopposed, but there would be much hard fighting in the months ahead for the Marines, plus the misery of Guadalcanal's steamy jungle climate. Most of the troops on both sides would suffer from malaria and other tropical diseases.

Losses	
U.S.:	1,596 killed, 4,183 wounded, about 5,000 malaria cases
Japanese:	At least 29,000 dead, unknown number wounded

Between August and October, Japanese and American warships battled in "the Slot," the body of water that separated Guadalcanal from the rest of the Solomons. The August 24 Battle of the Eastern Solomons between carriers was a United States victory.

Eventually the United States Navy gained the upper hand, while ashore, the Marines struggled to defend Henderson Field from determined Japanese attacks, and then to push the Japanese off the island completely. The Second Marine Division arrived to reinforce the First, and Army units landed in October, but it wasn't until early February 1943 that the remaining Japanese evacuated the island.

JAPANESE OPERATIONS JULY 1942–FEBRUARY 1943

ALLIED OPERATIONS JULY 1942–FEBRUARY 1943

IN THE SOLOMON ISLANDS
Japanese forces landed on Guadalcanal and New Guinea in July. In New Guinea, the Japanese failed to take Port Moresby, while on Guadalcanal they tried unsuccessfully to reinforce the island's defenders, after the United States' landings.

THE LEADERSHIP

VANDEGRIFT'S COMMANDERS included legendary Marines Lewis "Chesty" Puller, Evans Carlson, and Merritt "Red Mike" Edson. Vandegrift commanded until December, when Army general Alexander Patch took over.

ALEXANDER ARCHER VANDEGRIFT (1887–1973)
Born in Virginia, Major General Vandegrift had served in the Marine Corps for 33 years before taking command of the First Marine Division in early 1942. He won both the Navy Cross and the Congressional Medal of Honor for his "tenacity, courage, and resourcefulness" on Guadalcanal and became commandant of the Marine Corps in January 1944.

"We can hold."

—First Raider Battalion commander Merritt Edson, to headquarters during an attack on Henderson Field

HARUKICHI HYAKUTAKE (1888–1947)
Commander of the Japanese Seventeenth Army, General Hyakutake had hoped to fight in New Guinea and was disappointed that the Japanese high command gave priority to Guadalcanal. Unlike many Japanese generals in the Pacific, he survived the battle.

"Success or failure in recapturing Guadalcanal is the fork in the road which leads to victory for them or us."

—Japanese document captured on Guadalcanal

55

VICTORY IN THE DESERT

In June 1942, German General Erwin Rommel's Afrika Korps captured the seaport fortress of Tobruk. This opened the way for German and Italian tanks to rumble across the desert toward Egypt. Rommel forced the Allies to retreat so rapidly that he seemed to be invincible.

The Afrika Korps next faced the British Eighth Army at El Alamein, the gateway to Egypt and the Suez Canal. The Suez was a vital supply route for Allied forces. Before continuing his invasion, Rommel had to wait for the arrival of fuel and reinforcements. Meanwhile, Hitler promoted the triumphant commander to field marshal.

In August, General Bernard Montgomery took charge of the British Eighth Army and built up a powerful force of artillery, men, and new American tanks. His army included British, Indian, New Zealand, Australian, and South African troops.

On the night of October 23, Montgomery opened a thousand-gun artillery barrage on the Afrika

GERMAN ANTI-TANK MINE
The Axis and Allied forces at El Alamein laid mine fields to defend against attack. Anti-tank mines such as this one exploded when a tank passed over them. Before they could attack, Montgomery's men at El Alamein had to first clear the the mines defending Rommel's position. This was done by troops trained to find and destroy mines.

"DESERT RATS"
ROUT AFRIKA KORPS
A crewman of a German tank surrenders to charging British Eighth Army soldiers. The men of the Eighth Army won the nickname "Desert Rats" because of the harsh conditions they endured fighting in the North African desert.

Losses

Allies:	13,500 killed/wounded
Axis:	30,000 killed/wounded
	30,000 prisoners

Korps. In bright moonlight, the Allied tanks smashed through Afrika Korps defenses. The battle raged for ten days as Rommel fought desperately against overwhelming Allied firepower. He finally retreated, fighting his way back across 1,750 miles (2,835 kilometers) of desert. Burned-out Axis tanks and guns littered the route. The Afrika Korps suffered 60,000 casualties before reaching temporary safety in Tunisia.

Now, Egypt and Libya were securely in Allied hands. General Montgomery won wide fame as the commander who had defeated the once-unstoppable Rommel.

BRITISH 8TH ARMY OCTOBER 1942–FEBRUARY 1943

ROMMEL AVOIDS DESTRUCTION
As the victorious Eighth Army closed in, Rommel's army escaped through a gap and began a 1,750-mile (2,853-kilometer) fighting retreat. Rommel regrouped in German-controlled Tunisia.

THE LEADERSHIP

GENERAL BERNARD MONTGOMERY's daring leadership gave new confidence to an Allied army that had been forced on the defensive by brilliant German general Erwin Rommel.

BERNARD MONTGOMERY (1887–1976)
The British knew "Monty" as a tough disciplinarian and respected him for bringing them victory in North Africa. El Alamein was his greatest triumph. Montgomery would go on to work with American General Dwight D. Eisenhower during the invasion of Europe.

"I said that the mandate was to destroy Rommel and his army, and that it would be done as soon as we were ready. We are ready NOW!"

—Montgomery

"We hold the gateway of Egypt with full intention to act."

—Rommel

ERWIN ROMMEL (1891–1944)
By now, Rommel was known to Allied and Axis peoples alike for his many victories. Although Churchill publicly acknowledged Rommel as a great general, the prime minister was determined to defeat the "Desert Fox." Churchill dismissed British commanders until he found the confident Montgomery, who was willing to attack.

LIGHTING THE TORCH

The Allied invasion of French North Africa on November 8, involved 116,000 American and British troops. Some units departed from Britain, while others sailed from the U.S. The invasion, called Operation Torch, was organized into three separate forces at Casablanca in Morocco and at Oran and Algiers in Algeria. Because German-occupied France was officially an ally of the Nazis, some of the 10,000 French troops in the region fired on the British and Americans. Then a high-ranking French naval officer at Algiers, Admiral Jean Darlan, called on French troops not to resist the Allies. By November 14 Torch forces had pushed almost to the Tunisian border.

> *"The next beach you land on will be defended by the Germans."*
>
> —General George Patton scolds an American soldier taking a rest after landing in Operation Torch

ALLIED LANDINGS NOVEMBER 8, 1942
AXIS REINFORCEMENTS BY AIR

COASTAL LANDINGS The Allies landed on the coast of the French colonies of Morocco and Algeria. In most places, the French defenders did not fight hard against the Allied invaders.

THE LEADERSHIP

THE POLITICAL SITUATION in French-ruled North Africa gave Torch's commander, General Dwight Eisenhower, serious problems. The American dealings with Admiral Darlan, considered pro-German, were controversial.

JEAN DARLAN (1881–1942)
Commander of the French Navy at the outbreak of World War II, Darlan became one of the most powerful men in France after the armistice with Germany. He was assassinated in Algiers in December 1942.

READY TO GO
American troops aboard a landing craft prepare to hit the beach outside Oran. The troops wore shoulder patches showing the United States flag; it was hoped that the French would be less likely to fire on the invaders if they knew they were American.

Losses: November 8 Landings	
Allies:	856 killed, 837 wounded (approximate)
French:	700 killed, wounded unknown

ROMMEL STRIKES AGAIN

In early 1943, the war in North Africa seemed almost won, but there was a surprise in store for the Allies. When German armor shattered French units now fighting on the Allied side, Rommel gambled on an all-out attack. On February 14, his tanks smashed through the Atlas

> *"What was really amazing was the speed with which the Americans adapted to modern warfare."*
>
> —Rommel

Mountains at Kasserine Pass. He drove back the Americans, gaining 50 miles (80 kilometers) and beating off a counterattack. Kasserine was a defeat for the Americans, but not a disaster. Reinforced by British and French troops, U.S. forces held up the German advance. Rommel soon withdrew toward the Mareth Line, the main German defensive position in Tunisia.

▬▬▬ US Forces February 14–22, 1943
▬▬▬ Axis Attacks February 14–22, 1943

THROUGH KASSERINE
Rommel himself was in command of the panzers that broke into Kasserine Pass, a gap in the Atlas Mountains, on February 20.

THE LEADERSHIP

KASSERINE PASS WAS A FAILURE of leadership, although lack of experience in dealing with the Germans was a major factor, too. The defeat was a lesson for United States commanders.

LLOYD R. FREDENDALL (1898–1963)
Fredendall reportedly spent the weeks before Kasserine overseeing the building of his headquarters rather than arranging his forces to meet the German threat. Relieved of command, he was replaced by General George S. Patton.

HILLS OF TUNISIA
American infantry on the move in Tunisia. The rugged terrain gave the Allies one advantage: it forced German armor into narrow mountain passes, where tanks were vulnerable to the massed firepower of American and British artillery.

Losses

U.S.:	2,500 killed/wounded, 2,500 prisoners (approximate)
Axis:	2,000 killed/wounded/prisoners (approximate)

Rolling Back the Axis Powers

For the Allies, 1943 brought success in Europe and the Pacific. Soviet forces pushed the Nazis west and the United States fought steadily toward Japan. Still, the Axis powers were far from beaten.

On the Eastern Front, the Soviet Union dealt Nazi Germany a devastating defeat, capturing the German Sixth Army at Stalingrad in February. Then, in a massive tank battle at Kursk that summer, the Soviets shattered all German dreams of conquest. By the end of the year, the Soviet Army was prepared to advance into German-held Poland.

Allied commanders in the West were determined to break into German-occupied France, but there

MARINES IN THE SOLOMONS
United States Marines with dogs, used for scouting and running messages, start off for the jungle front lines on the island of Bougainville, in the Solomon Islands, in 1943.

January	February	May	July
Churchill and Roosevelt meet at Casablanca, Morocco	Japanese abandon Guadalcanal	German and Italian forces in North Africa surrender	Battle of Kursk
	German Kharkov offensive begins	Warsaw ghetto uprising put down	Allies invade Sicily
German army surrenders at Stalingrad			Mussolini's Fascist government falls

were not yet enough landing craft to invade across the English Channel. They decided to first make an offensive through southern Europe, which was not as strongly defended. The Allies invaded Sicily in July, then mainland Italy in September. A new Italian government soon forced Mussolini from power and made peace with the Allies, but German troops moved in, determined to stop the Allies in Italy.

In the Pacific, American forces fought toward Japan, moving island by island, battling Japanese defenders who bitterly contested every inch of island ground. Two skillful leaders commanded separate forces moving against Japan: through the Southwest Pacific came General Douglas MacArthur, attacking by way of New Guinea and the Philippines, and across the Central Pacific came Admiral Chester Nimitz.

INVADING ITALY
American troops go ashore in Italy. The vessel at left is an LST (Landing Ship, Tank), one of the many specialized craft that allowed tanks and other vehicles to land directly on open beaches.

TEHERAN CONFERENCE

During the war the leaders of the Allied nations met to decide military strategy and discuss political matters. A major conference took place in Teheran (Tehran), Iran, from November 28 to December 1, 1943. At Teheran, Stalin pushed for the opening of a "second front" in Europe to take some of the pressure off the Soviet Army. Churchill and Roosevelt agreed to invade France in 1944 while the Soviets pushed westward toward Germany.

THE "BIG THREE" AT TEHERAN
The "Big Three" met only twice—here at Teheran and at Yalta, in the Crimea. From left to right: Stalin, Roosevelt, Churchill.

August	September	November	December
Soviets retake Kharkov	Allies invade Italian mainland Italy surrenders to Allies	Soviets retake Kiev Teheran Conference	U.S. General Dwight D. Eisenhower named supreme commander for upcoming invasion of France

SECURING NEW GUINEA

Although the campaign on Guadalcanal was one of the most famous, the American-Australian campaign to drive Japanese forces

"It may truthfully be said that no air commander ever did so much with so little."

—Army Air Forces commander Henry "Hap" Arnold, on General George Kenney

from New Guinea was just as long and hard-fought. By January 1943 the Allies had retaken Papua (the eastern half of New Guinea), but the Japanese made a last-ditch effort to reinforce their outposts on the rest of the island. On March 2–3, however, United States and Australian bombers caught the Japanese fleet in the Bismarck Sea, sinking troop transports carrying 7,000 men, as well as four destroyers.

■■■ **ALLIED OFFENSIVES**
JUNE 1943–APRIL 1944

■■■ **JAPANESE RETREATS**
SEPT. 1943–MARCH 1944

FIGHT FOR NEW GUINEA
From the island of New Guinea the Japanese might be able to launch an invasion of Australia. To stop this threat the Allies attacked New Guinea and the nearby Japanese-controlled island of New Britain.

THE LEADERSHIP

ADMIRAL YAMAMOTO WAS DETERMINED to reinforce New Guinea, even though General Kenney's Allied planes had control of the air. The Japanese called the resulting disaster the "Bismarck Sea Massacre."

GEORGE C. KENNEY (1889–1977)
General Kenney became MacArthur's air commander in August 1942. Kenney revolutionized air force tactics in the Pacific by insisting that pilots attack ships from low altitudes using machine guns and bombs, instead of bombing from high altitudes. This new technique was effective in the Battle of the Bismarck Sea.

Losses: New Guinea Campaign

Allied:	2,850 killed
Japanese:	12,000 killed

ABOVE THE CLOUDS
A Navy bomber attacks Japanese ships in the Bismarck Sea, in March 1943. American airpower smashed a fleet of Japanese troop ships and destroyers sent to reinforce Japanese forces in New Guinea.

A RACE FOR PALERMO

On July 10, 150,000 troops of General George Patton's U.S. Seventh Army and General Bernard Montgomery's British Eighth Army began landing at two separate points on the island of Sicily's southern coast. British and American airborne forces dropped inland by parachute and glider. Conquest of the island was complete by August 17, but the main Axis forces escaped capture. The Germans had skillfully evacuated most of their forces (40,000 Germans and 60,000 Italians) across the Strait of Messina to the Italian mainland.

"We're not interested in holding on to anything except the enemy."

—Patton to reports that troops were holding their position

ALLIED OPERATIONS JULY–AUG. 1943

GERMAN RETREAT AUGUST 13–17, 1943

SICILIAN OFFENSIVE
The Allies invaded the island of Sicily, at the tip of the Italian peninsula. Axis troops escaped to mainland Italy, where they prepared to resist the coming invasion.

HERMANN GÖRING

ARMBAND
worn by German troops defending Sicily

THE LEADERSHIP

PATTON AND MONTGOMERY WERE BOTH AMBITIOUS soldiers with a thirst for fame. Their advances toward Palermo, Sicily, became a race between U.S. and British forces. Patton won.

GEORGE S. PATTON, JR. (1889–1945)
Patton was as famous for his flamboyant personality as he was for his skill as a commander. In a legendary performance, he led a rapid Allied drive across France, then into Germany in 1944–1945.

SICILIAN WELCOME
The Italian people were war-weary. The Italian troops defending Sicily offered little resistance, and the civilian population happily greeted the Allies. The two German panzer divisions on Sicily, however, fought hard.

Losses

Allies:	22,800 killed/wounded/missing
Axis:	165,000 killed/wounded/ missing/prisoners

63

CITADEL AT KURSK

Despite the setback at Stalingrad, the Wehrmacht still managed to mount a major offensive in February 1943. By April German forces had retaken Kharkov from the Soviets and reached the Donets River.

To the north, German forces moved back from Moscow to form a better defensive line. These movements left a vulnerable bulge in the Soviet lines, centered on the city of Kursk. Field Marshal Erich von Manstein planned an operation, code-named

Citadel, that was aimed at slicing off this bulge and destroying the Soviet Army forces inside it.

The Germans, however, had to wait three months for the spring thaw and to assemble as many tanks as possible. These included powerful new models like the Panther Mark V.

The German delay gave the Soviets time to prepare their defenses. Hundreds of thousands of civilians dug

PANZER JACKET
This double-breasted jacket was worn by Germans of all ranks fighting in panzer divisions. The jacket had a close-fitting design, with concealed buttons, to make it easy for the tank operator to move around.

German Imperial Eagle insignia

DESTROYED TANK
A wrecked German panzer at Kursk. By now the Soviets had huge numbers of tanks, including the powerful T-34, which many historians believe was the outstanding tank of the war.

Losses	
Soviet:	178,000 killed/wounded/missing/prisoners
Axis:	56,000 killed/wounded/missing/prisoners

4,000 miles (6,480 kilometers) of trenches and anti-tank ditches. The Soviet Army laid more than a half-million anti-tank mines and prepared to fire close to 10,000 artillery pieces and rocket launchers.

In July, the Wehrmacht struck the Kursk Bulge. Some German units made good progress, but the well-prepared Soviet defenses soon stopped the Wehrmacht advance. Then the Soviet forces launched a huge counterattack that lasted from July 12 to August 5, with tanks battling at close range.

The largest tank battle in history ended with the Germans withdrawing westward and with the Soviet Army in pursuit. By the time the German forces halted on the Dnieper River in September, the Soviets had retaken Kharkov and Smolensk.

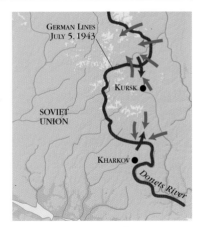

▬▬ GERMAN ATTACKS JULY 1943
▬▬ SOVIET COUNTERATTACKS JULY 1943

A WEAK POINT IN THE SOVIET DEFENSE
The bulge at Kursk went 100 miles (162 kilometers) into the German lines. The German commanders hoped to cut off the Soviet troops defending this large area.

THE LEADERSHIP

AT KURSK, THE RUSSIAN GENERALS WON a great victory. General Pavel Rotmistrov and others had defeated famous panzer leaders like General Heinz Guderian and General Hermann Hoth.

HERMANN HOTH (1885–1971)
General Hoth made his reputation as a skillful panzer commander in the 1940 Battle of France and later led the Fourth Panzer Army in the unsuccessful attempt to relieve the trapped Sixth Army at Stalingrad. After being defeated at Kursk he was recalled by Hitler.

"[The Soviet tanks] scurried like rats across the battlefield."
—Guderian on the Battle of Kursk

PAVEL ROTMISTROV (1901–1982)
In the Battle of Kursk, General Rotmistrov led the Fifth Guards Army (Armored), one of the Soviet Army's elite units. Promoted to field marshal, he became deputy commander of all Soviet armored formations.

"The earth was black and scorched with tanks like burning torches."
—Rotmistrov on the Battle of Kursk

ITALIAN AVALANCHE

On September 3, General Bernard Montgomery's British Eighth Army landed in Calabria on the Italian mainland. Six days later, the Allied Fifth Army, commanded by

> *"We don't give another inch. This is it! Don't yield anything. We're here to stay!"*
>
> —Clark to the troops at Salerno

United States general Mark Clark, began Operation Avalanche—a landing at Salerno, south of the vital port city of Naples. The German Tenth Army raced south in an effort to drive the Allies back from the beaches into the Mediterranean Sea. The Germans almost succeeded. Only massed firepower from ships, artillery, and aircraft—plus a parachute drop to reinforce the beachhead with airborne troops—held off two German panzer divisions.

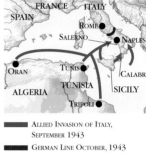

ALLIED INVASION OF ITALY, SEPTEMBER 1943

GERMAN LINE OCTOBER, 1943

WAR FOR PORTS
The Allies in Italy needed good ports because of the long supply lines from Britain and the United States.

THE LEADERSHIP

WHEN CLARK'S FORCE did not move fast enough after landing at Salerno, German defenders almost trapped the Allies on the beach.

MARK W. CLARK (1896-1984)
In a secret mission before Operation Torch, General Clark had landed in North Africa by submarine to negotiate with French officers controlling French colonies in North Africa. After Salerno, he remained in command of the Fifth Army in Italy through September 1944, and he accepted the surrender of German forces in Italy in May 1945.

BATTLE OF THE BEACHHEAD
Infantrymen of the British X Corps come ashore at Salerno, protected by a smokescreen. An army "corps" had two or three divisions. The British and Americans landed on separate beachheads with a river between them.

Losses

Allies:	15,000 killed/wounded/ missing/prisoners
Axis:	8,000 killed/wounded/ missing/prisoners

MARINES TAKE TARAWA

The first major operation of Admiral Chester Nimitz's Central Pacific campaign took place in November 1943, when United States forces landed on Makin and Tarawa in the Gilbert Islands. Makin fell easily, but the Marine landing on Tarawa on November 20 was another matter. Many landing craft grounded on a reef, leaving the Marines to wade in under heavy Japanese fire. The survivors were pinned down on the beachhead. Reinforced the next day, the Marines took the island by November 23. Both sides suffered terrible casualties. All but 17 Japanese troops were killed.

A million men cannot take Tarawa in 100 years."

—Admiral Keiji Shibasaki, Japanese commander in the Gilbert Islands

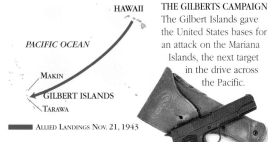

HAWAII

PACIFIC OCEAN

MAKIN

GILBERT ISLANDS

TARAWA

ALLIED LANDINGS Nov. 21, 1943

THE GILBERTS CAMPAIGN
The Gilbert Islands gave the United States bases for an attack on the Mariana Islands, the next target in the drive across the Pacific.

UNITED STATES M1911A1 PISTOL

THE LEADERSHIP

DETERMINED GENERAL JULIAN SMITH and courageous unit commanders like Colonel David Shoup of the Second Marine Regiment enabled the Marines to accomplish their mission at Tarawa.

JULIAN SMITH (1886–1975)
Soft-spoken General Smith commanded the Second Marine Division from May 1943 through April 1944 and was a veteran of Marine campaigns in the Caribbean and Central America. He went on to command all Marine units of the United States Navy's Third Fleet. After the war Smith commanded the Marine training center at Parris Island, South Carolina.

Losses	
U.S.:	1,000 killed, 2,000 wounded
Japanese:	All but 17 of 5,000 killed

HARD LESSONS
Taking cover behind a bullet-shattered palm tree, a Marine takes aim on Tarawa. The battle taught the Marines lessons in island fighting that they would put to good use in later operations.

D-Day, Leyte, and Liberation

As 1944 began, Axis forces were on the defensive from Russia to Greece, Italy to the South Pacific. Massive Allied offensives were launched to liberate Axis-occupied countries.

The Allies forced their way through Italy and captured Rome in early June. Italy surrendered, but German troops stubbornly kept fighting. On the eastern front, the siege of Leningrad ended as the Soviets drove the Nazis back. Soviet troops finally entered Germany itself in October.

In the Pacific, United States forces continued to island hop, moving closer to Japan with every island taken. The U.S. Navy led the way to winning back the Pacific. The Battle of the Philippine Sea in June was the greatest carrier engagement of the war. The Japanese fleet retreated after heavy losses. American troops invaded the Philippines

INDIAN TROOPS FIGHT IN BURMA
Sikh troops of the Seventh Indian Division, part of the famous British Fourteenth Army, are shown in action at Ngakydauk Pass, Burma, 1944. The Sikhs were some of the 2.5 million Indians who served in World War II; 380,000 Indians were killed or missing by the end of the war.

JANUARY	FEBRUARY	JUNE	JULY
Landing at Anzio	Allies stopped at Cassino	Allies liberate Rome	Breakout of Normandy at St. Lô
Siege of Leningrad ends		D-Day, Operation Overlord	
		Marines attack Saipan	
		Battle of Philippine Sea	

in October. Meanwhile, the navies fought the Battle of Leyte Gulf. The result was a decisive Japanese defeat. Japanese forces were now on the defensive throughout the East, as the British fought to win back Burma and Chinese forces in China battled the Japanese invaders.

To defend against invasion from Britain, Hitler had built the "Atlantic Wall." This line of heavy guns and concrete bunkers stretched along the coasts of France, Belgium, and the Netherlands. On June 6, "D-Day," the Allies attacked this wall, sending a massive invasion force onto the beaches of Normandy, France. The Allies broke through German defenses, liberating Paris that August. In December, the Nazis counterattacked in the Battle of the Bulge, the final German offensive of the war.

INVADING THE NORMANDY SHORE
Americans wade toward the beaches from their landing craft during the invasion of Normandy on June 6.

RESISTANCE FIGHTERS

Armed opposition to Hitler's rule gained strength in Nazi-occupied Europe. "Resistance" fighters secretly fought the enemy wherever they could. Military trains were blown up, sentries killed, and downed Allied fliers rescued. Using short-wave radios, the Resistance reported on enemy military movements. Resistance members were executed if caught. When Allied troops arrived in France, breaking into Hitler's Europe, the forces of the Resistance rose up to join them.

DUTCH RESISTANCE ARMBAND

LIBERATING FRANCE
A member of the Resistance cooperates with an American soldier during a street fight in a French city. French resistance fighters, called the "maquis," fought bravely against the Nazi occupier.

AUGUST	SEPTEMBER	OCTOBER	DECEMBER
Allies liberate Paris	V-2 rockets fired at London	MacArthur returns to the Philippines	Battle of the Bulge
		Battle of Leyte Gulf	

UP THE BOOT OF ITALY

The Allied Fifth Army captured Naples in September 1943, but the advance up the "boot" of Italy was difficult and bloody. This mountainous region greatly favored the German defenders, commanded by Field Marshal Albert Kesselring. He established defensive lines across the width of the Italian peninsula. When Allied forces broke through one line, Kesselring would withdraw his forces and set up a new one. Italy's rugged mountain chains and fast-flowing rivers slowed the Allied advance.

In January the Allies began "Operation Shingle." The plan was to make an "end run" around the German defensive line by landing a force at Anzio, just south of Rome. Then the Allies would move to take Rome, Italy's capital. The Sixth Corps, commanded by United States general John P. Lucas, went ashore on January 22. Lucas achieved surprise, and the landing was unopposed. Still, the Germans had time to assemble a force and trap the Allies on the beachhead.

ASSAULT RIFLE
The FjG42 rifle issued to German paratroopers could fire single shots, or automatically, like a machine gun. It was an advanced weapon for its time, but was difficult to manufacture and was not used widely.

MUD AND COLD
For the foot soldier, Italy was a miserable place to fight. In some battles, casualties from cold and wet weather were greater than combat losses. Here, American GIs try to free a jeep from thick mud.

Losses: Italian Campaign	
Allies:	312,000 killed/wounded/ missing/prisoners
Axis:	536,000 killed/wounded/ missing/prisoners

behind the invasion beaches. Meanwhile, 2,483 ships carrying 131,000 American, British, and Canadian troops crossed the English Channel. Starting at 6AM, some 4,000 landing craft began carrying the troops ashore.

British and Canadian forces landed on the beaches code-named Gold, Juno, and Sword and quickly overcame the German defenses. So did the American Seventh Corps on Utah Beach. But on Omaha Beach, the American Fifth Corps landed in a hail of German fire. They suffered heavy casualties but fought hard and managed to secure the beach.

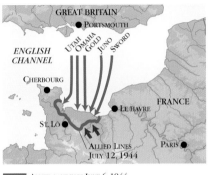

ALLIED LANDINGS JUNE 6, 1944

GERMAN COUNTERATTACKS JUNE, 1944

CROSSING THE CHANNEL
The five landing beaches in France extended across 60 miles (97 kilometers) of Normandy coastline. Parachute and glider landings were made behind the landing zone.

ON THE BEACH AT NORMANDY
Combat engineers clear the beach of obstacles while landing craft unload. A barrage balloon floats above one of the ships. Barrage balloons trailed steel cables to entangle enemy aircraft that tried to make low-level attacks.

Losses: June 6	
Allies:	2,500 killed, 8,050 wounded/ missing/prisoners
Axis:	6,500 killed/wounded/ missing/prisoners

RED ARMY HITS BACK

In January 1944, Soviet troops lifted the siege of Leningrad, where at least a million inhabitants had died of cold, hunger, and disease since German

> *"[Germans] who did not want to give themselves up died on the spot."*
>
> —Zhukov describing a Soviet attack in Operation Bagration

troops had surrounded the city in August 1941. In June 1944, just after the Allied landings in Normandy, a Soviet force of 1.2 million men began Operation Bagration, a massive offensive named for a great nineteenth-century Russian general. In six weeks, the Soviets smashed the Wehrmacht's Army Group Center and pushed the German lines back 300 miles (483 kilometers). In terms of casualties, it was a worse defeat for the Germans than Stalingrad.

GERMAN LINES JUNE 23, 1944

BERLIN ●
GERMANY
SOVIET UNION
RUMANIA
ITALY

BAGRATION Soviet forces assembled for Operation Bagration stretched from the Baltic Sea in the north to the Carpathian Mountains in the south.

▬▬ SOVIET OFFENSIVES JUNE–DEC. 1944
▬▬ GERMAN LINES DECEMBER 15, 1944

THE LEADERSHIP

SOVIET COMMANDERS USED HEAVY CONCENTRATIONS of troops to punch holes in the German lines. This was the same tactic used by the Germans in the Blitzkrieg campaigns of 1939–1940.

KONSTANTIN ROKOSSOVSKY (1896-1968)
Once considered an enemy of Soviet leader Stalin, Marshal Rokossovsky fought brilliantly during the battles of Moscow, Stalingrad, and Kursk. He planned Bagration and commanded the First Byelorussian (Belarussian) Front in the operation, winning promotion to field marshal.

ROLLING WEST
Soviet armored forces move forward in Lithuania. The Soviet Army included units of what it called "tank-landing troops"—infantry who rode into battle aboard tanks.

Losses

Soviet:	Unknown, but in the hundreds of thousands
Axis:	350,000 killed/wounded/prisoners

JAPANESE FIGHT TO THE LAST

After taking the Gilbert Islands, the next American objectives were the Marshall Islands, then the Marianas—Guam, Tinian, and Saipan. Air bases on these islands would put American bombers in range of Japan. On June 15, American forces attacked Saipan, finally winning on July 9. At the same time, navy pilots triumphed in the Battle of the Philippine Sea, June 19–20. The Americans shot down nearly 500 Japanese warplanes and sank three aircraft carriers. After more heavy fighting, Guam and Tinian were secured by August. Soon the first United States B-29 bombers flew from the Marianas to hit Japan.

"Whether we attack, or whether we stay where we are, there is only death."

—Japanese general Yoshitsugo Saito, on Saipan

THE MARIANAS
United States forces captured the Mariana Islands, which gave a base from which to bomb Japan and prepare for an invasion of the Philippines, 1,500 miles (2,414 kilometers) to the west.

■ ALLIED OPERATIONS JUNE–JULY 1944

THE LEADERSHIP

JAPANESE NAVAL COMMANDERS GAMBLED by launching a major carrier operation in the Battle of the Philippine Sea. The United States Navy, under Admiral Marc Mitscher, defeated the Japanese offensive.

HOLLAND M. SMITH (1882-1967)
General Smith was nicknamed "Howlin' Mad" for his fierce temper. He was overall commander in the Gilbert Islands in 1943 and oversaw the Marianas campaign in 1944. By the time he retired in 1946, Smith had spent 41 years in the Marine Corps.

GRENADE ATTACK
Marines throw grenades at a Japanese position. Saipan's 50 square miles (81 kilometers) were honeycombed with caves and bunkers, which the Marines and soldiers had to take one by one.

Grenade launcher

Japanese hand grenade

Losses	
U.S.:	14,111 killed/wounded
Japanese:	29,000 killed, 1,000 prisoners

FRANCE IS FREE

By June 26, three weeks after D-Day, 25 Allied divisions were ashore in France. Despite the success of the Normandy landings, the Allied forces had difficulty breaking out of the beachhead. Normandy farmland was crisscrossed by "hedgerows" of earth, rocks, and trees that made excellent defensive positions for German machine guns and tanks. Clearing the hedgerows was a tough process. Finally, in late July, General Patton's Third Army blasted out of

Normandy with help from heavy bombers. German losses in tanks and men were severe in this action, known as the Battle of St. Lô.

On August 15 the Allies launched Operation Dragoon—a second invasion of France—with landings in the south on the Mediterranean coast. Dragoon forces then began moving to link up with the Allies in the north.

FREE FRENCH PATCH
This patch was one of several worn by Free French forces. It features the Cross of Lorraine, a traditional symbol of France.

Losses: Breakout from Normandy	
Allies:	36,976 killed, 172,696 wounded/prisoners
Axis:	240,000 killed/wounded, 210,000 prisoners

PARADING AMERICANS
Victorious Americans parade through Paris, passing the Arc de Triomphe, a monument to French military victories. The honor of being the first Allied force to enter liberated Paris went to a Free French division.

Paris fell to the Allies on August 25.

On September 4, General Montgomery's British forces captured the Belgian port of Antwerp. This city was of great value when Canadian forces secured the banks of the Scheldt River, which connected the city to the sea. This was another slow and costly operation.

The Allied drive across France slowed as the armies ran out of fuel and supplies. Later in September, the Allies began Operation Market-Garden, an attempt to break into Germany through the Netherlands. Although American and British airborne troops captured bridges over the Rhine River, the armored forces were unable to link up with them, and the operation failed. By the end of the year the Allies halted before the West Wall, the last defensive line protecting Germany.

THE NORMANDY BREAKOUT
Allied units broke out of Normandy in all directions, moving south to take coastal ports, and northeast toward Belgium. Another Allied force landed on the coast of southern France and began a drive north to Germany.

■■■ ALLIED OPERATIONS AUGUST–DEC. 1944

■■■ GERMAN LINES DECEMBER 15, 1944

THE LEADERSHIP

GERMAN LEADERS SUCH AS ROMMEL and Rundstedt urged Hitler to make peace with the Allies, who were victorious everywhere. The German commander in Paris, Dietrich von Choltitz, even disobeyed Hitler's order to destroy the city.

OMAR N. BRADLEY (1893-1981)
Known as the "Soldier's General" for his close relations with the troops, Missouri-born Bradley commanded the First Army at Normandy. He next led an army group—more than 1.3 million men—across France and into Germany. He was one of only five generals promoted to five-star rank in the army.

"Bravery is the capacity to perform properly even when scared half to death."

—Bradley

DIETRICH VON CHOLTITZ (1894-1966)
A former panzer general, Choltitz found himself in command of the German garrison in Paris just a few weeks before the Allies reached the city. He surrendered Paris, then spent two years in Allied captivity.

"Is Paris burning?"

—Hitler, following up his order to destroy the city

RETURN TO THE PHILIPPINES

In September 1944, United States forces landed in the Palau Islands, the last island chain before the Philippines. It took the First Marine Division and army units more than two months of constant combat to capture the island of Peleliu. This was one of the costliest operations in the Pacific war.

Admiral Nimitz and General MacArthur then joined forces to liberate the Philippines from Japanese occupation. In October, a United States invasion fleet of 750 ships and 160,000 troops steamed into Leyte Gulf.

The Japanese saw an opportunity to destroy the invasion fleet and cripple the United States Navy in the Southwest Pacific. The plan was to send a carrier force to lure the American Third Fleet into battle, while a second Japanese force moved in to destroy the invasion's transport vessels. The Third Fleet was led by Vice Admiral William Halsey, commander of the Allied South Pacific Forces.

The Japanese plan almost worked. Halsey's 64 ships did move north to defeat the carrier force, but the Battle of Leyte Gulf—the biggest naval battle in history—ended in a decisive victory for the United States

JAPANESE SAILOR'S HAT
This Japanese naval cap was worn by an aircraft mechanic. The cap protected the sailor from summer sun.

Anchor symbol marking this hat as property of the Japanese Imperial Navy

Losses: Land Campaign, Leyte	
U.S.:	15,500 killed/wounded/missing
Japanese:	70,000 killed/prisoners

DRAMATIC RETURN
MacArthur had a flair for publicity. This photograph of him wading ashore from a landing craft onto the beach at Leyte, the Philippines, won him much admiration.

Navy. Though there were heavy American losses, submarines and the planes of small carriers saved the invasion transports by fighting off the Japanese fleet of Vice Admiral Takeo Kurita.

Large numbers of Japanese troops remained in the Philippines, however, and they fought with determination. Japanese forces on the large Philippine island of Leyte counterattacked American-held airfields in December 1944, but were defeated. In January 1945, with Leyte finally secured, the American Sixth Army landed on Luzon, the biggest Philippine island. The capital, Manila, fell in February, although fighting continued until the final Japanese surrender.

LEYTE GULF
The Japanese fleet was to hit the American invasion fleet by sailing through the San Bernardino Strait, north of Leyte, while the Second Attack Force came up from south of Leyte by way of the Surigao Strait.

▬▬ ALLIED OPERATIONS OCT.–DEC, 1944

▪▪▪▪ JAPANESE NAVAL FORCES OCT., 1944

▪▪▪▪ U.S. NAVAL FORCES OCT., 1944

THE LEADERSHIP

SOME HISTORIANS QUESTION whether Vice Admiral Halsey should have gone after the Japanese carriers, leaving the invasion transports weakly protected. Japanese Vice Admiral Kurita would later be faulted for not defeating the invasion.

WILLIAM F. HALSEY, JR. (1882-1959)
"Bull" Halsey graduated from Annapolis, served in World War I, and earned his wings as an aviator before taking part in many major naval operations in the Pacific during World War II. He ended the war as a five-star admiral.

"To the people of the Philippines: I have returned."

—MacArthur, October 20, 1944

TAKEO KURITA (1889-1977)
Like Halsey, Vice Admiral Kurita fought in many Pacific campaigns, from Java in 1942 through the Mariana Islands in 1944. His flagship was sunk beneath him during the Battle of Leyte Gulf, but he was rescued.

"Would it not be shameful to have the fleet remain intact while the nation perishes?"

—Kurita, to naval headquarters, before Leyte Gulf

CRISIS IN THE ARDENNES

As the winter of 1944–1945 set in, Germany was under constant attack as the Allies advanced on all fronts. And yet Hitler believed victory was still possible. He gambled on a great offensive through the Ardennes in Belgium—the same rugged, forested region that had served as the gateway for the invasion of France in 1940.

German armor would drive a wedge between the American and British forces and capture the Belgian city of Antwerp. The Ardennes Offensive, Hitler believed, would lead the Western Allies to seek a peace settlement. That would leave Hitler free to throw all his strength against the Soviet Army in the East.

After assembling a force of 250,000 men with strong armored forces, the Germans struck on the morning of December 16. They attacked a lightly defended section of the American line, creating a bulge that gave the struggle its nickname: the Battle of the Bulge. The Wehrmacht made good progress at

SUBMACHINE GUN
The "Schmeisser" nine-millimeter MP-40 submachine gun was one of the standard German small arms of the war. It fired 500 rounds a minute.

FIERY ASSAULT
An American tank burns as Wehrmacht infantry advance on the first day of the Ardennes Offensive. The Battle of the Bulge was the biggest engagement ever fought by the American Army.

Losses: December 16–January 16	
U.S.:	19,000 killed, 15,000 prisoners
German:	100,000 killed/wounded/missing/prisoners

first. Many American units were made up of inexperienced replacements, who panicked as the panzers appeared. Poor weather grounded Allied aircraft, helping the Germans.

In many places, however, American troops bravely held their ground and slowed the German advance. The 101st Airborne Division was surrounded at Bastogne, a vital road junction, but held on until George Patton rushed his Third Army north in support.

By the beginning of January the German offensive was halted, and by the end of the month American and British forces had destroyed or captured the attackers.

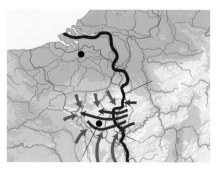

▬▬▬ GERMAN OFFENSIVE DEC. 16, 1944–JAN. 1, 1945
▬▬▬ ALLIED COUNTERATTACKS DEC., 1944–JAN., 1945

PUSHING BACK THE BULGE
Patton's Third Army attacked the "Bulge" from the south, while British units to the north joined in and reinforced defenses along the Meuse River. By January 8, the bulge was gone, and the Allied line was where it had been in early December.

THE LEADERSHIP

THE SUDDEN GERMAN ATTACK brought out the best and worst in the American leadership. Some unit commanders performed poorly, but the actions of General Bruce Clark at St. Vith and General Anthony McAuliffe at Bastogne saved the day.

HASSO VON MANTEUFFEL (1897-1978)
A highly decorated panzer commander who fought in both North Africa and Russia, General Manteuffel commanded the Fifth Panzer Army. This unit caused the most damage to the Allies in the Bulge. After the war he was active in German politics.

"I have made a momentous decision. I will go over to the offensive—out of the Ardennes, with the objective Antwerp."

—Hitler, September 16, 1944

ANTHONY C. MCAULIFFE (1898-1975)
An artilleryman, General McAuliffe was acting commander of the 101st Airborne during the division's defense of Bastogne. His defiant reply to a German demand for surrender made him famous. In the 1950s he commanded United States forces in Europe.

"'Nuts!'...In plain English, it means go to hell."

—Colonel Joseph Harper, relaying McAuliffe's reply to a surrender demand

81

The Final Struggle: A Year of Victory

As the Allied powers approached victory in the spring of 1945, they suffered a great blow. President Franklin D. Roosevelt died suddenly, leaving Vice President Harry Truman to take office.

In Europe, Germany was caught between the Western allies and the Soviets. The Soviets brought widespread death and destruction as they advanced westward through Poland and into Germany. Wehrmacht forces fought to allow civilian refugees to escape the Soviet army's invasion.

In the West, the Allies rolled eastward to meet the Russians on the Elbe River in April. Hundreds of thousands of German troops laid down their arms. Berlin fell to Soviet forces on May 2, two days after Hitler killed himself in his bunker beneath the wrecked city. German forces formally surrendered on May 8, called "V-E Day," for "Victory in Europe."

NEW AND TERRIBLE BOMB
An American B-29 crewman snapped this photo of the mushroom-shaped cloud from the explosion at Nagasaki.

January	February	April	April (continued)
Soviet troops take Warsaw, Poland	Yalta Conference	Franklin Roosevelt dies; Harry Truman becomes president	Red Army begins Berlin offensive
Soviets liberate Auschwitz concentration camp	Allied bombing destroys Dresden, Germany	Allies cross the Rhine	Battle of Okinawa begins
	U.S. forces land on Iwo Jima		Hitler commits suicide

Japan, however, showed no sign of quitting, even though its navy was almost destroyed and bombing had turned many of its cities to rubble. Allied forces island-hopped ever closer to Japan. Japanese defending the islands of Iwo Jima and Okinawa made the Americans pay in blood for every yard of ground.

The war against Japan ended suddenly. On August 6 an American B-29 bomber dropped a new and fearful weapon—the atomic bomb—on Hiroshima. The bomb destroyed the city in an instant. A second atomic bomb was dropped on Nagasaki three days later. On August 15, Japan's Emperor Hirohito announced that his nation would seek peace terms. On September 2, the surrender ceremony took place on the deck of the battleship *Missouri* in Tokyo Bay. World War II was over.

PREPARING FOR INVASION

American warships in Japanese waters, August 1945. If Japan had not surrendered, the Allies would have landed on Kyushu, Japan's southern home island. Military planners expected the battle for Japan would have cost at least 250,000 American lives.

THE DIVINE WIND

In late 1944, many Japanese pilots made suicide attacks. They were members of a special attack corps known as the "divine wind," or kamikaze. The kamikazes intentionally crashed their aircraft into Allied ships, sinking many and killing thousands of sailors. The term "divine wind" came from a legendary storm that wrecked an invading Mongol fleet in the 13th century. Now the Japanese pilots hoped their violent sacrifice would stop the American advance.

BOUND FOR DEATH

Kamikaze pilots pose for a portrait before their mission. Almost 1,000 kamikazes attacked American ships at Okinawa.

May	June	July	August
Berlin falls	Allied occupation of Germany officially begins	First atomic bomb tested	Atomic bombing of Hiroshima and Nagasaki
Germany surrenders		Potsdam Conference	Japan surrenders
		Okinawa secured	

RED ARMY TAKES BERLIN

By the beginning of 1945 Soviet forces had driven the Germans from Yugoslavia, Romania, and Bulgaria. German troops were gone from Greece and Albania as well.

The Germans tried to stop the Soviets at Budapest, the capital of Hungary, but that city fell in February. In the north, Germany ally Finland wanted to make peace.

The Soviet army now moved in for the kill. On January 12–14, two huge Soviet offensives began rolling westward, through East Prussia and into the German heartland. These forces were the First Ukrainian Front, commanded by

Marshal Ivan Konev, and the First White Russian Front, commanded by Marshal Georgi Zhukov.

By the end of the month the Soviet Army reached the Oder River, less than 50 miles (81 kilometers) from Berlin. While Konev and Zhukov paused to prepare for the final assault on Berlin, Soviet forces to the south conquered Hungary. In April, the Soviets took Vienna, the Austrian capital.

Cloth made from synthetic fibers and recycled wool

GERMAN FIELD JACKET
In the Battle of the Berlin, the Wehrmacht had few soldiers left to fill its uniforms. This jacket was worn by a German soldier in the last days of the war.

RED FLAG OVER BERLIN
Triumphant Soviet troops raise their red flag over the Reichstag, the German capital building. This historic moment symbolized victory in a conflict that had claimed 20 million Soviet lives and left much of their homeland in ruins.

Losses	
Soviets:	300,000 killed/wounded/missing
German:	1,000,000 killed/wounded/missing (civilian and military)

On April 22 the great Battle of Berlin began. The Soviets battered the city with more than 12,000 artillery pieces and 21,000 rocket launchers. The armies fought bitterly, making their way through the city block by block. From a secret bunker in Berlin, Hitler gave orders to his last troops that they should fight to the death. Many Nazis did just that, but by the end of April only a few government buildings in the center of the city remained in German hands. As the Soviets took Berlin, Adolf Hitler committed suicide on April 30.

On the afternoon of May 2, the Soviet flag flew over the Reichstag, the German capital building.

▬▬▬ SOVIET OFFENSIVES JANUARY–APRIL, 1945
▬▬▬ GERMAN LINES MAY 7, 1945

THE UNSTOPPABLE SOVIET ARMY
The 1945 Soviet offensives were a two-front attack. As Zhukov and Konev advanced to encircle Berlin, another Soviet army to the south captured Budapest. Taking Hungary opened the way into Austria and Czechoslovakia.

THE LEADERSHIP

THE SOVIET ASSAULT ON BERLIN was also a race between commanders. Marshals Zhukov and Konev disliked each other, and each wanted the glory of conquering Berlin. In the end, Stalin ordered Konev to halt, giving Zhukov the honor of taking the city.

IVAN S. KONEV (1897–1973)
Konev made his reputation during the Soviet battle for Ukraine and western Russia in 1944. After the war, he saw his rival, Zhukov, fall out of favor with the Soviet government. Konev continued to hold important commands until the early 1960s.

"I think it's going to be quite a fight."
—Stalin to Zhukov before the Battle of Berlin

HEINRICH HIMMLER
Himmler was an early member of the Nazi Party and helped build Hitler's fanatic bodyguard, the SS (*Schutzstaffel*). In 1944, Hitler put him in charge of Germany's eastern defenses, where he was captured and committed suicide. Had Himmler survived, he would have been tried and executed for his role in Nazi war crimes.

"It is all finished. Death will be a relief to me. I have been deceived and betrayed by everyone."
—Hitler, April 29, 1945

UNCOMMON VALOR

Japan still had an army of 2 million men in early 1945, many of them in China. There, Japanese forces launched an offensive against the Nationalist capital, Chungking (Chongqing). With United States help, the Chinese halted that offensive. Meanwhile, to the south, the British Fourteenth Army was pushing the Japanese out of Burma. The Burma Road, the vital supply route to China, reopened in late January.

The United States now moved to take the Ryukyu Islands to prepare for the invasion of Japan. On February 19, three Marine divisions landed on Iwo Jima. This volcanic island had little natural cover, and the Japanese had built strong defenses. Iwo Jima was taken by March 16, with a loss of 6,821 Marines killed and 20,000 wounded.

FLAG OF THE RISING SUN
Its silk fabric stained with blood, this Japanese flag was taken as a grim war trophy by a Marine who fought at Iwo Jima. Iwo Jima was the Marines' costliest battle; a third of the Marines killed in World War II were killed there.

Losses: Okinawa
U.S.: 12,500 killed/missing, 36,800 wounded
Japanese: 110,000 killed, 7,400 prisoners
Okinawan civilians: At least 70,000 killed

FAMOUS FLAG-RAISING
Marines raise the American flag over Mount Suribachi, Iwo Jima, on February 23. Associated Press photographer Joe Rosenthal took this photograph, one of the best-known images of the war. Three of the flag-raisers would be killed before the island fell.

On April 1, a fleet of 1,300 ships put two Marine and two army divisions ashore on the much larger island of Okinawa. The last major battle in the Pacific, the struggle for Okinawa also proved to be the costliest for the United States. While soldiers and Marines fought their way across the island, 1,000 kamikaze aircraft swarmed down on the American ships offshore. The Japanese also sent the *Yamato,* the world's largest battleship, into battle against the invasion fleet, but torpedo bombers sank her.

Japanese suicide attacks sank 31 ships and killed 5,000 sailors, the United States Navy's worst single-battle loss of the war. Okinawa finally fell on June 21.

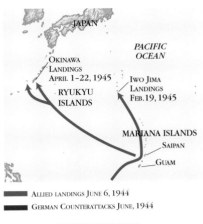

ALLIED LANDINGS JUNE 6, 1944

GERMAN COUNTERATTACKS JUNE, 1944

TOWARD JAPAN, THE FINAL PUSH
United States forces moved north from the Mariana Islands against Okinawa and Iwo Jima in the Ryukyu Islands. Okinawa was only 350 miles (563 kilometers) from Kyushu, the southernmost of Japan's home islands.

THE LEADERSHIP

JAPANESE GENERAL TADAMICHI KURIBAYASHI led the defense of Iwo Jima. General Mitsuru Ushijima commanded at Okinawa. American Marine general Harry Schmidt led the attack on Iwo Jima.

SIMON BOLIVAR BUCKNER (1886-1945)
The son of a Confederate Civil War commander, General Buckner was in charge of American forces assaulting Okinawa. He was killed during the battle, the highest-ranking American field commander to die in World War II.

"Among the Americans who served on Iwo Island, uncommon valor was a common virtue."

—Admiral Nimitz

SOEMU TOYODA (1885-1957)
Admiral Toyoda became commander in chief of the Japanese fleet in March 1944. He commanded in the Battle of the Philippine Sea. During the battle for Okinawa, Toyoda ordered a massive kamikaze attack on the American fleet.

"It is very likely that our enemy… will attack us soon in their expedition to invade Japan."

—General Tadamichi Kuribayashi, Japanese commander at Iwo Jima

THE BRIDGE AT REMAGEN

After recovering from the Battle of the Bulge, the Western Allies again started an advance toward the Rhine River. This great natural barrier protected Germany from the west.

Early in March eight Allied armies, totaling about 4 million men, approached the Rhine's western bank. The Germans had blown up most of the bridges crossing the river, but on March 7 the United States Ninth Armored Division discovered a railroad bridge still standing at Remagen, Germany. The Germans had failed to destroy it.

The American First Army crossed the bridge and gained a foothold on the other side. The Germans managed to destroy the bridge with artillery and bombs, and it finally collapsed 10 days later, but the Rhine defenses had been breached.

The main cross-Rhine assault came on March 23, starting with massive Allied bombing and shelling. Two paratroop divisions dropped behind the German defenders, while American, British, and Canadian troops crossed over. A week later 325,000 German soldiers surrendered in the

VOLKSSTURM-GEWEHR 1-5
This inexpensive automatic weapon was manufactured for the *Volkssturm*—the "People's Army." This organization was made up of old men and young boys, Germany's last-ditch defenders.

CROSSING UNDER FIRE
American soldiers take cover as best they can while crossing the Rhine. Despite the pre-crossing bombardment, many units came under heavy German fire. The small assault boats used to ferry infantry across the river did not offer much protection.

Losses: for April 1945	
Allies:	26,969 killed/wounded
Axis:	1,650,000 killed/wounded/ prisoners (most prisoners)

Ruhr region of Germany and the local commander, Field Marshal Walter Model, committed suicide.

On April 25, the spearhead of the American Ninth Army reached the Elbe River. This was the border dividing the Western and Soviet zones of operation. Meanwhile, General Montgomery's forces battled through northern Germany, and Patton's Third Army drove into southern Germany, Czechoslovakia, and Austria.

In some places, such as the Hartz Mountains, there was still much hard fighting, but by the beginning of May the Wehrmacht collapsed. On May 7, Field Marshal Alfred Jodl signed a surrender document at Eisenhower's headquarters in Reims, France.

▬▬▬ ALLIED OPERATIONS MARCH–MAY, 1945
▬▬▬ GERMAN RUHR "POCKET" APRIL, 1945

INTO THE GERMAN HEARTLAND
In the spring of 1945 Allied armies drove through German defenses. Thousands of German prisoners were taken in the Ruhr region.

THE LEADERSHIP

WITH THE ALLIED CROSSING OF THE RHINE, German leadership in the west approached collapse. All but the most fanatic German commanders knew the war was lost and surrendered to the Allies.

JACOB L. DEVERS (1887-1979)
General Devers commanded Allied forces in Operation Dragoon, the invasion of southern France in August 1944. Next, he led the Sixth Army Group, consisting of the American Seventh and French First armies, advancing into Germany. He later served as Commander of United States Army Ground Forces.

"While the bridge [at Remagen] lasted, it was worth its weight in gold."

—General Walter Bedell Smith, Eisenhower's chief of staff

ALFRED JODL (1890-1946)
Wounded in World War I, Jodl considered giving up his military career and studying medicine, but he stayed in the German army. Marshal Jodl owed his rank to his Nazi Party membership and friendship with Hitler. Convicted of war crimes, he was executed after the war.

"With this signature the German people and the German Armed Forces are...delivered into the hands of the victors."

—Jodl on signing the surrender document

89

THE FIRST NUCLEAR BOMBS

Soon after World War II began, scientist Albert Einstein informed President Franklin Roosevelt that "extremely powerful bombs of a new type" could be constructed. Einstein said "the element uranium may be turned into a new and important source of energy in the immediate future." He knew that Germans were making progress in atomic science, and he feared what would happen if the Nazis developed such a terrible weapon.

In June 1942, the United States Army Corps of Engineers began the "Manhattan Project"—the secret name for research into making a nuclear bomb. Because of the difficulty of producing such a weapon, the Manhattan Project required a major industrial effort and the brainwork of top scientists. All this had to be done in complete secrecy. For that reason, much of the scientific work took place at Los Alamos, a remote outpost in New Mexico.

UTTER DEVASTATION

The destructive power of the Hiroshima bomb was equal to 20,000 tons of TNT. It was reported that nothing was left standing or alive within three quarters of a mile from the center of the blast. Many thousands would later die of radiation poisoning.

MANHATTAN PROJECT PATCH

The secretary of the army authorized this shoulder patch for the Manhattan Project's military personnel in 1945. The project was known officially as the "Manhattan Engineer District of the U.S. Army Corps of Engineers."

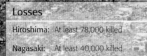

Losses	
Hiroshima:	At least 78,000 killed
Nagasaki:	At least 40,000 killed

On July 16, 1945, the scientists at Los Alamos exploded a test nuclear bomb at New Mexico's Alamogordo Air Base. By August there were two bombs—a uranium bomb, code-named "Little Boy," and a plutonium bomb, code-named "Fat Man." Vice President Harry Truman had taken office when President Roosevelt died in April. Hoping to stop the war in the Pacific, Truman gave permission to use these bombs against Japan.

On August 6, a United States B-29 bomber dropped "Little Boy" on Hiroshima, destroying the city. This bomb was 2,000 times more powerful than any bomb ever used. Truman called on Japan to surrender. When no reply came, "Fat Man" was dropped on Nagasaki on August 9. Six days later Emperor Hirohito announced that Japan would seek peace.

• • • • • U.S. BOMBER ROUTES FROM TINIAN
✸ ATOMIC BOMB ATTACKS

THE TWO CITIES
The city of Hiroshima, Japan, was the first target for nuclear bombing. The city of Kokura was the intended target for the second bomb, but poor weather forced the American pilots to switch their mission to Nagasaki.

THE LEADERSHIP

J. ROBERT OPPENHEIMER WAS SCIENTIFIC HEAD of the Manhattan Project. General Leslie R. Groves was officer-in-charge. Groves advised Truman to drop the bomb, though several scientists objected to the destruction it would cause.

HIROHITO (1901-1999)
Emperor Hirohito was considered divine, a "god-king," by the Japanese, who would fight to the death to keep him on the throne. All military orders were issued in the emperor's name. Real government power, however, was held by the military. Hirohito's actual role in the war is not fully known.

"The enemy has begun to employ a new and most cruel bomb…"

—Hirohito's radio broadcast to his people after the atomic bombing

LESLIE R. GROVES (1896-1970)
A graduate of the Massachusetts Institute of Technology, Groves oversaw construction of the Pentagon in 1940. In the Manhattan Project, Groves managed 129,000 personnel. He later worked for a defense contractor, the Remington Rand Corporation.

"The shock waves from the detonation could crush your plane. I can give you no guarantee that you will survive."

—J. Robert Oppenheimer to *Enola Gay* crewmen who would drop the bomb on Hiroshima

THE CAPTAINS OF WAR

AXIS LEADERS

PIETRO BADOGLIO
Headed Italy's armed forces, 1925–1940; led Italian government after fall of Mussolini.

SHIGEYOSHI INOUYE
Vice admiral; commanded Japan's Fourth Fleet, the "South Seas Force"; led Japanese offensive against New Guinea.

WILHELM KEITEL
Member of the General Staff in World War I; chief of staff of the German military high command, 1942–1944.

GUNTHER H. VON KLUGE
Field marshal; commanded in Poland, France, Russia; part of 1944 plot to kill Hitler; committed suicide.

WALTHER MODEL
Made field marshal in 1944; commander in chief in West, 1944; committed suicide in 1945.

JISABURO OZAWA
Vice admiral; commanded Japan's Combined Fleet in 1945; defeated in Battle of Leyte Gulf.

ERICH RAEDER
Grand Admiral of German Navy, 1928–1943; resigned in 1943; sentenced to life in prison after the war.

TAKEO TAKAGI
Rear admiral; won Battle of Java Sea; commanded in Battle of Coral Sea; killed at Saipan.

TOMOYUKI YAMASHITA
General; captured Singapore in 1941; commanded in Philippines 1943–1945; executed for war crimes.

ALLIED LEADERS

HENRY H. "HAP" ARNOLD
West Point; U.S. Army Air Forces commander in chief during the war; later First General of the Air Force.

THOMAS A. BLAMEY
Commanded Australian forces in the Middle East and Pacific; first Australian field marshal.

CHIANG KAI-SHEK
Led Chinese Nationalists, 1928–1949; ruled Taiwan after Communists took power in China.

HENRY D. CRERAR
Chief of Canadian Army General Staff; led Canadian First Corps, then First Canadian Army with distinction.

CHARLES DE GAULLE
Leader of Free French forces after the fall of France; became president of France three times, 1945–1969.

MILES DEMPSEY
General; commanded corps in British Eighth Army, 1942-1944; led British Second Army into Germany.

ROBERT L. EICHELBERGER
West Point; general; commanded U.S. First Corps in Pacific, and U.S. forces in occupied Japan.

COURTNEY H. HODGES
General; took over U.S. First Army after Omar Bradley; first Allied commander across the Rhine.

ERNEST J. KING
Annapolis; commander in chief of the U.S. fleet after Pearl Harbor. Planned U.S. offensive in the Pacific.

ALLIED LEADERS

THOMAS C. KINKAID
Annapolis; captain of the USS *Indianapolis,* 1937, rose to vice admiral commanding U.S. Seventh Fleet in Pacific.

WALTER KRUEGER
General; veteran of Spanish-American War and World War I; commanded U.S. Sixth Army, 1943–45.

CURTIS E. LEMAY
General; former fighter pilot; developed tactics for air power and strategic bombing in Pacific.

JOHN C. H. LEE
West Point; general in charge of U.S. Army Service of Supply (SOS) in Europe. Organized massive build-up of supplies before D-Day.

GEORGE C. MARSHALL
Virginia Military Institute; U.S. Army chief of staff during World War II; called America's "Organizer of Victory"; became U.S. secretary of state.

WILLIAM SLIM
General; led British Fourteenth Army in Burma; field marshal and Chief of Imperial General Staff after war.

BREHON SOMERVELL
West Point; head of U.S. Army's Service of Supply; played major role as chief of logistics.

CARL A. SPAATZ
West Point; commanded U.S. air forces in Europe and, later, Japan. Oversaw strategic bombing of Europe.

RAYMOND A. SPRUANCE
Annapolis; admiral; commanded U.S. Fifth Fleet in the Pacific; directed Gilberts, Marianas, and Ryukyu campaigns.

JOSEPH W. STILWELL
West Point; commander of U.S. forces in China-Burma-India Theater of War; worked with Chinese and British forces to defeat Japanese.

INDEX

ACKNOWLEDGMENTS
Media Projects, Inc. and DK Publishing, Inc. offer their grateful thanks to: Clifford J. Rogers, Associate Professor of History, United States Military Academy; Steve R. Waddell, Associate Professor of History, United States Military Academy; Stuart A.P. Murray; artist and collector Don Troiani, Historical Art Prints, www.historicalartprints.com; Erika Rubel; Ron Toelke, cartography; Rob Stokes, relief mapping and cartography.

Photography and Art Credits
(t=top; b=bottom; l=left; r=right; c=center; a=above)
AKG-London: 32, 34. **akg-images**: 42–43b.
AP/Wide World Photos: 20, 65l, 93cl. **Bildarchiv Preussischer Kulturbesitz**: 14b. **Courtesy of René Chartrand**: 9b. **Corbis**: 27l, 45, 62b; Bettmann 7t, 9t, 36; Hulton-Deutsch Collection 15r, 52l, 81.
The Illustrated London News Picture Library: 7b, 41l. **Imperial War Museum**: 2–3 (TR1156), 5t, 5cl, 6t (NAM212), 12t (CH192), 12–13b (MH13154), 14t, 17b (FLM1461), 19b (STT914), 22b (HU55640), 24l (MH13143), 24r (D1417), 25b (C5422), 26 (E1579), 28t (HU39577), 28–29b

(E2885), 30b (MH5588), 31l (E3230E), 40b (K974), 43c, 47b (OEM1566), 53c, 53b (TR1156), 56t, 56b (E18654), 58b (A12661), 64b (RR1885), 66b (NA6630), 68 (IND2994), 69t, 73 (EA26941), 74b (NYP30679). **The Mariners' Museum, Newport News, VA**: 16b. **National Archives**: 1, 8r, 9r, 13r, 15l, 16l, 16l, 18l, 18b 19l, 21l, 21r, 23l, 23r, 27r, 29t, 31b, 33cl, 33b, 35l, 35b, 37l, 37r, 38l, 38r, 39, 41r, 42t, 43r, 44l, 44r, 46t, 46b, 47t, 48, 49t, 49b, 50, 51cl, 51br, 52r, 54b, 55l, 55r, 57l, 57r, 58l, 59l, 59b, 60t, 60–61b, 61t, 62r, 63l, 63b, 65r, 66t, 67cl, 67b, 68–69b, 69cr, 70b, 71l, 71r, 72l, 72r, 74t, 75t, 75b, 76b, 77l, 77r, 92All, 93tl, 93tr, 93cl, 93c, 93cr, 93bl, 93br, 94All.
Courtesy of Don Troiani www.historicalartprints.com: 4t, 4b, 5cr, 5br, 17t, 19r, 24t, 30t, 32t, 35t, 37t, 40t, 51tr, 54t, 63r, 64t, 67tr, 70t, 75cl, 76t. **Courtesy of the U.S. Navy**: 93tc, 93bc.

Cover Credits:
Imperial War Museum: front tla, back c, front flap, back flap. **Library of Congress**: front cl, front br. **Courtesy of the National Museum of the U.S. Army**: front c.